**Speaker's Corner Books**

is a provocative new series designed to stimulate,
educate, and foster discussion on significant public
policy topics. Written by experts in a variety of
fields, these brief and engaging books should be
read by anyone interested in the trends and issues
that shape our society.

Social Security and the Golden Age:
An Essay on the New American Demographic
George McGovern

TABOR and Direct Democracy:
An Essay on the End of the Republic
Bradley J. Young

Think for Yourself!:
An Essay on Cutting through the Babble, the Bias, and the Hype
Steve Hindes

Two Wands, One Nation:
An Essay on Race and Community in America
Richard D. Lamm

One Nation Under Guns:
An Essay on an American Epidemic
Arnold Grossman

For more information, visit our Web site,
www.fulcrumbooks.com

The Solution Is You!
An Activist's Guide

Laurie David

 Fulcrum Publishing
Golden, Colorado

Library of Congress Cataloging-in-Publication Data
David, Laurie.
 Stop global warming : the solution is you! / Laurie David.
    p. cm. -- (Speaker's corner books)
  ISBN-13: 978-1-55591-621-3 (pbk. : alk. paper)
  ISBN-10: 1-55591-621-X
 1. Global warming--Prevention--Citizen participation. 2. Environmental protection--Citizen participation. 3. Greenhouse effect, Atmospheric. 4. Environmental education--United States. 5. Environmentalists--United States--Anecdotes. I. Title.
  QC981.8.G56D38 2006
  363.738'74525--dc22

                         2006024786

Printed in Altona, MB, Canada, by Friesens Corporation
0 9 8 7 6 5 4 3 2

Editorial: Sam Scinta, Katie Raymond
Design: Jack Lenzo
Cover image: Mark Seliger
The blogs featured in the book first appeared on HuffingtonPost.com.

Fulcrum Publishing
4690 Table Mountain Drive, Suite 100
Golden, Colorado 80403
800-992-2908 • 303-277-1623
www.fulcrumbooks.com

For my two daughters, Cazzie and Romy,
future activists.

For Larry, who told me it would be a lot easier to
try to change the world than to change him.

For John Adams, Natural Resources Defense Council
founder, who guided me to this problem and has
been leading the way for more than thirty years.

And for Al Gore.

"God gave Noah the rainbow sign,
No more water, the fire next time."
—Spiritual Song

Contents

Foreword

Thirteen years ago, I met a materialistic, narcissistic, superficial, bosomy woman from Long Island. She was the girl of my dreams. She read People *magazine, watched hours of mindless television, and shopped like there was no tomorrow. Finally, I'd met someone as shallow as me. I was hopelessly in love. We got married in a touching ceremony in Las Vegas. The cabdriver who witnessed it was deeply moved. But then, after a few short months, I began to sense that something had changed. She started peppering her conversation with words like* ozone layer, sustainable forestry, *and* toxic runoff. *The very mention of the word* diesel *would bring on back spasms. I began to notice new people hanging around the house, people who were not in show business and wore a lot of tweed. Clearly, something was amiss. She was growing. How hideous. But what was now all too painfully obvious was that I, Larry David, the shallowest man in the world, had married an environmentalist.*

I wrote and performed that more than six years ago at the behest of my wife, who was producing a fund-raiser for the Natural Resources Defense Council. It was the first of many favors she's asked me to do on behalf of her environmental work—all unpleasant—culminating in this, the foreword to her book. Who even reads forewords? I know I go right to chapter one. If I wanted to read something by the person who wrote the foreword, I'd buy their book. I could be out golfing now, or shopping for an electric wheelchair.

So, having to write this is exactly the kind of thing I've been doing since she became an activist. It never ends.

Fund-raisers, speeches, TV interviews, not to mention all the indignities I'm forced to endure in my house on a daily basis, such as having to use postconsumer recycled toilet paper, the sort of thing you might find in a Greyhound bus terminal or on a whaling vessel. As a result, I am no longer able to sit for more than ten minutes at a time and can barely bring myself to attend movies or sporting events. Of course, brushing my teeth and showering raise issues about the amount of water I use. My showers are down to a minute and a half, and I've had to forego the conditioner. What used to be a ritual I enjoyed and luxuriated in now feels like I'm on amphetamines, a whirling dervish of arms and legs, desperately trying to finish within my allotted time.

But it's out of the house where I've begun to fear for my safety, as she has a very short fuse when it comes to environmental transgressions. She's castigated swarthy gardeners in my presence for using leaf blowers, while I stood behind her trying to convey through mime that she and I aren't that close. The mere sight of a Hummer often triggers fits and seizures—and I was forced to install a special seat belt that crisscrosses on the passenger side to keep her from harming herself.

A few weeks ago, I came home and found a camera crew from *Oprah* in the living room interviewing her. As soon as I arrived, they slapped a microphone on me and then bombarded me with questions about the environment, which I faked my way through as if I was filling up a blue book on a college exam. I've never failed to walk away from any of these interviews without thinking my career was over.

Once, I came home from playing golf to find her planted in the doorway, arms akimbo, blocking my path. "What are you doing?!"

"What?"

"Don't you dare come in here. You've got pesticides on your shoes. Those golf shoes cause cancer. I don't want them in my house!"

But the worst of it was the night I got a call at work. It was ten o'clock. I was doing a rewrite.

"Your wife is on the phone!"

"Yes?"

"Mitsubishi's building a salt mine in San Ignacio."

"Honey, I've got a show tomorrow."

"Didn't you hear a word I said? They're endangering the gray whale!"

For the next two years, I couldn't have one conversation without hearing the word *Mitsubishi*. She was obsessed with Mitsubishi. She'd go up to strangers on the street: "Don't buy anything from Mitsubishi. They're killing the whales!"

Then she dragged me down to San Ignacio to see the whales. For three days, I slept in a tent, drank from a canteen, and conducted my business in an outhouse. She actually got to touch a whale and had her first orgasm in years.

But the coup de grâce was when I walked into my office and my assistant asked me what I was doing about a new car. I said I wasn't doing anything, the one I had was just fine. Then she proceeded to inform me that my wife had given away my Prius to the person who recruited the most people to sign up for her Stop Global Warming Virtual March Web site. I loved that car. I called to protest, but had to get through a maze of assistants to even get her on the phone. When I talk to her now, I have to get my information out very quickly, as if I'm talking to a doctor or an agent.

Of course, I wound up giving her the car. She's charming and persistent, and impossible—not just for me, but for anyone—to turn down. She's a gal on a mission. Better do what she says, so we can get on with our lives.

—Larry David

Introduction

I am a global warming activist, and hopefully by the time you finish reading this book, you will be one, too. In fact, I'm guessing you are already an environmentalist, even if you don't call yourself one yet.

Maybe that's because it has become so common to associate the word *environmentalist* with such derisive terms as *tree hugger* or *spotted-owl lover*—as if caring about trees and animals is a bad thing. But whether you are a Democrat or a Republican, a Christian, a Jew, or an atheist, you undoubtedly want and need clean air and clean water, both of which are basic inalienable rights for you and your children. You may love swimming in the ocean, walking in the woods, just being outside on a beautiful spring day. Such desires are neither Liberal nor Conservative. They're simply human. And environmentalism is the protection of those basic things. That is the accurate definition, and therefore my thesis holds: we are all environmentalists.

> "I am joining the hundreds of thousands who shall be marching in this Virtual March to demonstrate the concern that we all hold for the future of our planet and all the living things—flora, fauna, human, and animal—that exist upon it. The governments of the world have tarried long enough, and the United States is scarcely without doubt the greatest culprit among them. We the people have the strength to bring our country from our weak-kneed stumbling gait in the last ranks of reason to the leadership of the great march to environmental victory."
> —Walter Cronkite

This is the same conclusion that many great astronauts have come to after gazing at Earth from outer space. The man who holds the record for the farthest distance a human has traveled from the planet, Captain Jim Lovell of *Apollo 13*, has said: "When I circled the moon and looked back at Earth, my outlook on life and my viewpoint of Earth changed. You don't see Las Vegas, Boston, or even New York. You don't see boundaries or people. When viewed in total, Earth is a spaceship, just like *Apollo*—and just like *Apollo*, the crew must learn to live and work together. We must learn to manage the resources of this world with new imagination." *Discovery* commander Eileen Collins, the first female leader of a space shuttle, used her recent moment in the stratosphere to send a very strong message back to Earth, stating that she could see with her own eyes widespread environmental destruction, and warning that greater care was needed to protect our home. "The atmosphere almost looks like an eggshell on an egg, it's so very thin," she said. "We know that we don't have much air—we need to protect what we have."

Global warming is threatening that fragile shell and has now become the most urgent problem of our lifetime. Everything we know and love is at risk if we continue to ignore the warnings. This is not just my opinion, but that of the world's most respected scientists, the most cautious group of individuals on the planet. And although they have been largely ignored for the last two decades—and, worse, muzzled or rewritten by members of past and current administrations—their consensus opinion is that we now have less than ten years to slow global warming ... or else we set ourselves on a course we will not be able to correct. James Hansen, a revered climate scientist and director of the Goddard Institute for Space Studies at NASA, recently told me, "We are already guaranteed two more degrees of warming, but *we dare not go*

"Along with the public welfare and our individual freedoms, stewardship and protection of these natural resources should be at the heart of our political philosophy. What is leadership? For us (here in the U.S.) to ignore and deny the international call for discussion and consensus on the environment is an essential failure in our role as world leaders. The world wants to bring human activity in line with the health of the planet. And we remain asleep at the wheel."

—James Taylor

above that." Believe me, this guy knows what he is talking about, and when he said this, it sent shivers up my spine. (An increase of just one degree could make the difference between everything staying frozen in your freezer or melting on the kitchen floor.)

What kind of world are we going to choose to live in? A world that is two degrees hotter than normal? Or a world that is three or five degrees hotter, the results of which are unimaginable. Dave Hawkins, head of the Natural Resources Defense Council's Climate Center, put it this way: "If you had a choice to be in a car crash going five miles per hour or one going fifty miles per hour, which would you choose?"

> "I won the title of Miss Rhode Island on Earth Day (talk about timing!), April 22, 2006. I ran for Miss Rhode Island because I thought we, as an environmental movement, needed to find new and creative ways to reach new audiences. As Miss Rhode Island, my platform is 'Go Green! Global Warming Awareness.'"
>
> —Allison Rogers

Will we do what is necessary to avert the collision ahead?

The Science Is In

We, Americans, are the world's biggest contributors to global warming pollution—yet we are doing the least about it. In fact, we are barreling heedlessly in the wrong direction. The fuel efficiency of our cars has regressed to the lowest rates in twenty years, largely thanks to the popularity of low-mileage, high-emissions SUVs. We are continuing to build carbon-spewing, coal-burning power plants that account for more than 40 percent of our greenhouse gas emissions, despite the fact that cleaner coal-production technology already exists. As a result, there is now more carbon dioxide (CO_2) in our atmosphere today than there has been in the last 650,000 years. Seventy million tons a day.

More CO_2 means more heat. More heat means warmer oceans. Warmer oceans are like steroids for storms. Higher temperatures also cause more droughts, heat waves, melting ice, and rising sea levels (which is bad for coastal cities, where 80 percent of the world's population lives). For example, Hurricane Katrina, initially a Category One storm when it passed Florida, quickly became a Category Five hurricane when it hit the abnormally warm waters off the Gulf of Mexico. Ninety-nine percent of the glaciers in Alaska are melting. Forest fires are becoming more common, because the three ingredients needed for large-scale burning—heat, drought, and dead trees—are on the rise, thanks to global warming.

"Global warming and the pollution and burning of fossil fuels that cause it are threats we see here in California and everywhere around the world. We have no choice but to meet this challenge."
—Governor Arnold Schwarzenegger

"You can cut all the flowers but you cannot keep spring from coming," wrote poet Pablo Neruda—but, sadly, that's not really true anymore. Winter warming in the Northeast is affecting such basic things as when flowers bloom, which impacts the bugs and the birds that depend on them—researchers from Cornell, Harvard, and the Smithsonian Institute have all found recent evidence that flowers' natural cycles are changing: they are blooming up to a week earlier than previous records show. Nature has things perfectly timed. When you change that clock, everything is impacted. Warming is affecting the flow of rivers and streams, which impacts fish and then the fishermen. Warmer winters have meant less snow—bad news for skiers and other winter-sports enthusiasts—but it also leads to more wildfires as snow melts earlier and dry seasons last longer.

Snowpack is the amount of yearly accumulation of snow at higher elevations, and it saves water when we don't need it in the winter for when we do in the spring. In the western states, 75 percent of the water supply comes from snowpack. Since 1950, spring snowpack has declined by as much as 60 percent. In the first half of 2006, the resulting dry conditions set off more than 50,000 wildfires, burning more than 3 million acres in the United States.* Since the late 1980s, the U.S. Forest Service has extended wildfire season by seventy-eight days due to longer, drier summers.

Global warming is clearly visible everywhere: in Ohio, where the maple trees are so confused by unseasonably warm winters that they bud too early for proper maple-syrup production; or in the Massachusetts lakes, upon which fathers, sons, and daughters have played ice hockey every winter for the past thirty years, but which haven't frozen for the past few. It was visible last winter in Washington State, where college students home for Christmas found their winter jobs at the local ski resort gone because of the lack of snow; in New

* According to the National Interagency Fire Center

York City, where a record-breaking blizzard fell one day and sixty-degree temperatures occurred the next. In Dallas, Texas, 104-degree record heat (and it was only April!) caused overloads to the power grid and outages with summer still months away. As scientists are quick to point out, no one weather event can be blamed specifically on global warming, but the overall pattern of extreme weather events are proof that it is here.

The changing climate is also affecting our animal kingdom, as the warming trends are screwing up life for animals and, in a few scary situations, driving species toward extinction. A study published in January 2006 in the journal *Nature* documented the extinction of at least sixty-five species of harlequin frogs and as many as 112 amphibian species that have been wiped out since 1980, and primarily blamed climate change for their demise. The lead researcher, J. Allen Pounds, says, "Disease is the bullet killing frogs, but climate change is pulling the trigger. Global warming is wreaking havoc on amphibians and will cause staggering losses of biodiversity if we don't do something first."

Things Go Better with Coke

December 2, 2005

Polar bears live in the Arctic and are totally reliant on sea ice, which is vanishing faster than previously expected. Bears are so confused by rapidly changing weather cycles, they are waking up too early and disrupting their entire life cycle. For every week of winter lost due to global warming, adult polar bears lose twenty-two pounds because their food supply is so scarce. And thinner bears mean fewer cubs. Starting to get the picture? Not very soft and cuddly, is it?

Penguins face a similar plight. A few years ago, when two giant icebergs broke off the Antarctic ice sheet, it blocked the route from their breeding colonies to their feeding areas. As a result, they had to walk an extra thirty miles to reach food—no small task given that a penguin's average speed is one mile per hour.

Maybe it's time for corporate America to consider protecting a species that has been such a profitable sales tool. They say things go better with Coke. For the sake of the penguins and the polar bears, let's hope so.

A 2004 study, also in *Nature*, coauthored by nineteen scientists from around the world, estimates that global warming will lead to more than a million species' extinctions by 2050. In Georgia, the state bird, the brown thrasher, may disappear altogether as warmer temperatures continue to affect its habitat. Butterfly populations are already falling to new lows because of the change in climate. Everything is at risk. In northern Alaska, walrus babies are being separated from their mothers and are drowning when the melting sea ice collapses beneath them. Polar bears, the icon of all things cuddly, soft, and warm—so beloved that their image is used to sell everything from Coca Cola to insurance—are also drowning, as they have to swim farther and farther out to sea in search of the ice that they use as a platform from which to dive and catch their food. And in a recent shocking discovery, polar bears, for the first time ever, have been observed resorting to cannibalism because they are starving.

Global warming is going to affect many things that we

Global Warming Comes to the Breakfast Table

February 16, 2006

After the warmest January on record, maple-syrup producers in Ohio were surprised to have recently discovered premature maple tree buds. Budding of maples at this early date is unprecedented and means that, for the first time in living memory, there will be little or no maple syrup from the trees of northeastern Ohio this year.

"My family has been making maple syrup on our farm since just after the Civil War, and it is abundantly clear to us that something is dreadfully wrong in the maple woodlots here," said Tony Logan, an Ohio resident. Discussions with other maple-syrup producers in the area confirm that the premature maple-budding phenomenon is an area-wide concern.

The shocking thing about this story is that it is not about snowmelt at the North Pole, but about the impact of global warming on a very American rite of spring. A budding maple tree in early February is bad news for the farmer—and for anyone who enjoys delicious "made in America" maple syrup on their pancakes. Imminent change is upon us—not just in Ohio and Alaska, but at breakfast tables all across the United States.

all hold dear yet take for granted. Snowy winters and kids coming in tired and wet from snowball fights may be remembered only in old photographs. The yearly changing of the fall leaves from green to red and gold may become a memory told to children by their grandparents. (Vermont just suffered its shortest and least colorful autumn foliage in memory.) Normal summer nights where the cool relief from the setting sun sets the mood for whiling away the evening hours on the porch will be replaced with summer evenings that are nearly as hot as summer days, with no relief in sight. (Your body needs the cooler temperatures of nighttime to recover from the heat of the day.) Heat waves are the single biggest cause of weather-related deaths, more than hurricanes, tornados, and storms combined. Insects and bugs will no longer be just an annoyance. They will become deadly killers carrying a whole host of new or formerly defeated diseases, such as encephalitis, malaria, and dengue fever. Ragweed and pollen counts are going to thrive and double as temperatures rise. (Maybe this is why asthma rates in the last twenty years have also more than doubled.) Duke University scientists report that poison ivy is already becoming more prolific and more allergenic as rising CO_2 levels speed the vines' growth and increase production of its rash-causing chemical, compounding its itchiness. The vines are also becoming so pervasive they are literally choking trees and forests. The penguin will live only in movies and DVDs. Our

> "I am marching so that my children will be able to share this beautiful world with *their* children. I am marching because I truly believe that if *we all* don't do something fast, our children will never know the same life I believe we have all come to take for granted!"
> —Christie Brinkley

> "People who don't believe global warming can yell about it as loudly as they want, but it doesn't change the fact that the overwhelming scientific evidence and even the administration's own State Department have proven this over and over again. We must act now with the rest of the world to curb emissions so that we can leave our children a safer, healthier planet."
> —Senator Barack Obama

ability to use the land to grow food will be severely affected as the heat sucks the moisture from the soil like lemonade through a straw. April showers will no longer bring May flowers, but instead floods and devastation. The Northeast just came through its worst rain in a century, causing massive evacuations and flooding. Scenes not unlike New Orleans after Hurricane Katrina were seen on the evening news, but this time it was Washington, D.C., Delaware, Pennsylvania, Massachusetts, and New Jersey. The ground became so saturated that a 100-year-old elm tree collapsed in front of the White House steps. Rain isn't just rain anymore; it's harder, faster, stronger. "Climatologists are stunned because no one projected the magnitude of the storms that we are seeing," said Paul Epstein of Harvard Medical School Center for Health and the Global Environment. Epstein sees a clear pattern: heavy rain events of more than two inches a day are up 14 percent, and storms dumping more than four inches a day rose more that 20 percent. While most of New England experienced extreme rainfall and flooding, 45 percent of the United States was in moderate to extreme drought! As much as it all sounds like a first draft for a science-fiction film, it is entirely true.

An Open Letter to Bill Ford

November 28, 2005

Dear Mr. Ford: You are spending an enormous amount of money on an ad campaign touting your company's commitment to "innovation" and "fuel economy"—but no one is taking you seriously. Let me explain why: as long as you continue to sue state governments for their heroic attempts at reducing global warming emissions, you will be viewed as the bad guy.

This is not about sacrifice, Mr. Ford. And it is not about Americans not being able to own SUVs or trucks. This is about change. Thirty-thousand Americans would still be employed this Christmas season if Detroit had had the vision others had a decade ago: to make cars that use less gas. A new study published this week in the journal *Science* confirms that there is more carbon dioxide in our atmosphere now than in the last 650,000 years. Doesn't that terrify you? It should.

Here are a few very cold, hard facts.

The Truth Matters

January 30, 2006

I couldn't agree with Oprah more: the truth matters. And how timely that fast on the heels of Oprah's public lashing of James Frey comes a story of lying, suppressing facts, and the intimidation of science. James Hansen, director of the Goddard Institute for Space Studies at NASA, is the latest whistle-blower to publicly complain of attempts by those in the Bush Administration to silence him on the very disturbing conclusions he is reaching about the speed with which global warming is progressing.

"In thirty years of experience in government," says Hansen, "I have never seen control to the degree this is occurring now. If we don't take action to stop global warming in the next ten years, there will be large long-term consequences." Apparently, NASA and the administration don't agree with that—even though part of NASA's mission statement includes the phrase "to protect our home planet."

Will Hansen's declarations get the same coverage as the Oprah Frey story did? After all, the lies in Frey's book pale in comparison to the silencing of an esteemed climate scientist whose research seeks to inform us all about the fate of our planet.

The truth does matter.

Cold, hard fact number one: 2005 was the warmest year on record. More than 200 heat records were broken in that year alone. But the first half of 2006 has already surpassed that, holding the distinction as the warmest year on average since the United States started keeping records in 1895. Why? Because as the CO_2 levels increase in the atmosphere, heat increases too. They go hand in hand, like a horse and carriage. CO_2, no matter its source, wraps around the planet equally and uniformly—sort of like when you open a perfume bottle in the middle of the room, the fragrance particles will eventually drift to all four corners. The thicker the CO_2 blanket, the more heat gets trapped inside with no escape. Susan Hassol, a climate expert, explained it to me this way: imagine that when you go to sleep at night, you put a few blankets on to keep warm. At some point during the night, you start to get hot, and in response to that, you kick the blankets off. But the Earth can't kick off the extra CO_2 blankets we've added, so the planet gets warmer and warmer. Arctic ice is one of the planet's natural air conditioners and because of warming, it is melting. We are messing with the natural thermostat of the Earth—when you do that, you mess with nature itself.

Cold, hard fact number two: We are the cause of global warming. We didn't do this intentionally, but we know now that our way of life is causing global warming to happen. Power plants and cars, factories and buildings, the way we live, the way we work, the way we play, charging our cell phones and iPods, running our dishwashers and washing machines—all our fossil-fuel energy use contributes to global warming.

Cold, hard fact number three: Hurricane Katrina is just a taste of what's to come if we don't immediately get on a path to change. No other issue is going to directly impact your lives or your future plans more than global warming—not social security, not terrorism, not Iraq. Author Bill McKibben says, "When historians look back in a century, the most important thing about our time will be that these were the

Katrina: The Unnatural Natural Disaster

September 12, 2005
As the country continues to dissect the recent natural disaster, we might want to start considering what about the disaster wasn't actually "natural" at all. Water temperatures in the Gulf of Mexico were "unnaturally" high. Human activity, the burning of fossil fuels, is causing global warming. Global warming is causing the oceans to warm.

Scientists studying global warming have been predicting a scenario awfully close to what we are witnessing now: catastrophic weather causing flooding of whole cities, millions of displaced people, widespread disease, bug infestations, food shortages, poor people hardest hit, public-health nightmares, economic crises. This is the face of global warming. This is the warning we are not heeding. England, Germany, France, and 150 other countries are listening. The United States is covering its ears. And for those who are saying that now is not the time to be talking about global warming—I couldn't agree more. The time was a decade ago—when scientists *first* started sounding the alarm.

years that the temperature began to spike sharply up—that the Earth's climate, stable on a global level throughout civilization, began very suddenly to shift. This issue is as morally urgent as the civil rights movement was to our parents' generation."

Cold, hard fact number four: We can solve this.

Okay, I'm in, I get it … but how can I possibly do something about so huge a problem? Al Gore addressed that sentiment beautifully in the film *An Inconvenient Truth*: "A lot of people go straight from denial to despair without pausing in the middle and doing something about it." And the middle is where we are right now. We can no longer sit back and hope that someone else is going to solve this for us, because if they were going to do something to stop global warming, we would already have tougher fuel-economy standards (even China has higher-mileage cars than we do); we wouldn't have an energy policy that continues to subsidize the polluting industries of oil and coal instead of the industries that need the incentives, such as wind, solar, and other promising renewable resources; we wouldn't be selling off our national forests to the highest-bidding developer or destroying what little wetlands we have left. Those wetlands sure would have come in handy as a protective barrier in Louisiana during Hurricane Katrina. Wetlands act like sponges to storm surges, soaking up their power so that by the time they reach inland population centers, their damaging winds and heavy rains are weakened significantly. Since 1930, almost 2,000 square miles of the Louisiana Delta have eroded away, and coastal Louisiana continues to disappear at a rate of 25 to 35 square miles annually—that's literally

> "We can't blow people's minds with our show if all of the seats in our theaters are under water! Global warming is a topic that crosses all boundaries: no matter where you live in the world, or what your political affiliation, global warming is a phenomenon that will affect you, your family, and your community. We are already bearing witness to its effects with things like extreme weather and ice cap reduction. We need to band together to try to do something about it!"
>
> —Blue Man Group

a football field every hour. We have an administration that releases censored and edited reports on "climate change" (the White House's preferred term since a pollster advised them that it sounded less scary), and the American people continue to be misinformed and unconcerned. The chairman of the Environment and Public Works Committee in the United States Senate, James Inhofe (R-OK), uses every opportunity to spout that "global warming is a hoax," completely ignoring the conclusions of the federal government's own scientists, including NASA, the Environmental Protection Agency, the National Oceanic and Atmospheric Administration, and the National Academy of Sciences. *Can you believe* this guy is chairing the committee!

> "I am marching for my hometown of Lake Charles, LA, which was hit hard by Hurricane Rita. I spent three weeks volunteering in local shelters after Katrina. After the first few days, I noticed that people in the shelters weren't talking about the storm anymore. They were coming to me and saying, "Tell me more about this global warming. What is it? How is it contributing to the intensity of these storms?" We have to put an end to the Category 5 denial of global warming in Washington."
>
> —Jerome Ringo

Singer/songwriter John Mayer has a theory that we are all holding on to our denial because if we face the truth, we would immediately be forced to acknowledge that we, as individuals, are doing nothing about it. A huge, bright, uncomfortable spotlight glaring on top of our heads. But that discomfort will be a picnic compared to what we will feel if we ignore the warnings. And to do nothing, once warned, is no longer denial; it's immoral. As Montana Governor Brian Schweitzer so clearly put it, "Unless you're living naked in a tree and eating nuts, you're part of the problem."

> "Admitting you have a problem is half the solution. Twenty years ago, I had the experience of standing in front of a glacier whose face was at the water's edge, waiting for an overhanging chunk of ice to crash into the water. When I went back 20 years later, I saw the effects of global warming in this same location: if a chunk of ice fell off this time, it wouldn't make it to the water even if it rolled a couple hundred yards. Global warming is real; I have witnessed its effects."
>
> —Jon Fishman

All the solutions already exist—and they are the very same things we should be doing anyway—to free ourselves from our insane addiction to oil, a resource that we don't have much of, yet we currently waste and which makes us dependent on countries that aren't very dependable. College students, moms, dads, citizens, all of us must face this problem now and make solving it an American priority. *Government doesn't change until people demand it.* We need some good old-fashioned moral outrage! Our scientists are all speaking with one voice, and now the American people must speak with one voice too.

Tom Friedman recently wrote in the *The New York Times*, "Green is the new red, white and blue," and I couldn't agree more. He also urged college students to take this issue on. He wrote, "C'mon, kids! Wake up and smell the CO_2! Take over your administration building, occupy your university president's office, or storm in on the next meeting of your college's board of trustees until they agree to make your school carbon neutral. And while you're at

---

Global Warming: We Still Have the Power to Choose

February 22, 2006
On Sunday, *60 Minutes* had a stunning report from the rapidly melting glaciers of Greenland. Indeed, they're melting so rapidly that minutes after filming his spot, the glacier the reporter was standing on crashed apart into the open sea. It made for a jaw-dropping piece of video. The conclusion of the segment was equally jaw-dropping in the way that it, by ending on a hopeless note, missed a chance to make a vital point.

The segment closed with climate expert Bob Corell saying: "Even under the best of circumstances, this natural system of a climate will continue to warm the planet for literally hundreds of years no matter what we do."

I'm pretty sure he was trying to say that we will be feeling the consequences of how much we have already warmed the planet for years to come. But the kind of world we will live in is a choice we still have the power to make. Will we live in a world that is two degrees hotter or a world that is five to ten degrees hotter? The difference between those worlds is enormous—with implications for us all that are truly unimaginable.
The choice is ours.

it, ban gas-guzzling Hummers from your campus as well."

The collective power of millions of students demanding action would put us over the tipping point to real change. The day will come when young people will assign blame for this problem, but by then, we will be at a point where little can be done. We must avoid that moment. That's where you come in.

> "When we make the effort to end global warming, we are in effect saving the world. There is not a single square foot of land that hasn't been adversely affected. It is everyone's responsibility to return the world to her original health and beauty."
>
> —Lollapalooza

But first, let me tell you where I came in.

NASA Suffers Another Blow
to Its Mission to Protect the Planet

July 24, 2006

It's not a presidential duty to fundamentally alter the mission of government institutions to conform to an ideological agenda or for the benefit of wealthy donors. Yet, time and again, President Bush has done exactly that.

The latest example comes at NASA, where the White House has quietly altered the mission statement of this forty-eight-year-old agency, eliminating language describing the most important aspect of its critical work—"to understand and protect our home planet."

It's truly chilling that they would do this, thinking that nobody would notice. Fortunately, Andrew Revkin of *The New York Times* did notice, and it landed on the front page of the paper Saturday.

Since the quiet change to the mission statement was made in February, funding for research of our home planet has continued to disappear from NASA's budget as Bush puts increased emphasis on returning to the Moon and putting men on Mars.

Is it acceptable to the American people who subsidize NASA's work that the care of our planet is no longer considered important?

NASA scientists have been repeatedly betrayed by this White House, which has run roughshod over their scientific pursuits and replaced them with political pursuits, military-minded space pursuits, and, most dangerously, delayed a strong response to global warming from our government, despite the urgent warnings coming from NASA's own scientists. Recent research from NASA's Goddard Institute director James Hansen indicates that we may have less than ten years to stop global warming before it's too late. Hansen has fought courageously to keep the administration's muzzle at bay and convey this vital information to the American people. But with this latest attack on NASA's mission statement and its budget, the job just got a lot harder.

What kind of message is this for the 19,000 employees of NASA who were not consulted on this and are just finding out now that the mission of the institution they work for no longer includes the protection and care of planet Earth? What is the message to the American people? What should our response be?

The Making of an Activist

Finding your passion and devoting your life to it is a gift. Of course, it's a process, it takes time, and it doesn't necessarily show itself from day one. My path is the perfect example of this. I had so many jobs along the way, jobs that at the time seemed completely unconnected to any great master plan, but now, looking back, make total sense.

When I graduated college, I only had a vague notion of what I wanted to do, but I knew it had to be something in the entertainment field. My career began in a strange place for someone to accomplish that: Cincinnati, Ohio, as a copywriter for a car dealership. (And how crazy that, years later, I would start my advocacy on global warming by attacking the low-mileage of SUVs and promoting the hybrid car.) Strange also because I knew next to nothing about cars and I didn't even have a driver's license at the time. That was my first lesson—never let knowing next to nothing stop you! And something else I've learned along the way is just because someone says no doesn't mean they are right. I'll give you a perfect example of this: the marketing report NBC did to test *Seinfeld* for the first time. The conclusion of the "polling" was that the characters were completely unlikable and the show had no real appeal. We've

> "We must demand a separation between oil and state. We can get off oil and slow down global warming. We can vote for leaders who care about protecting your health, air, and the environment. We can support nonprofits who are making a difference. We can be environmentalists. So, get educated. Stay educated. So we can think for ourselves. And join the fight to save this unique blue planet for future generations."
>
> —Leonardo DiCaprio

A Conflict of Interest in the Halls of Academia

To: University of Virginia Department of Environmental Sciences

Numerous media outlets reported that one of your professors, Dr. Patrick Michaels, has accepted upward of $150,000 from coal interests and coal-burning electric utility companies for his advocacy against the overwhelming scientific consensus on global warming.

Is this solicitation of funds from industries that pollute the atmosphere with greenhouse gases in line with the university's mission?

Is it your policy to allow your science professors to openly solicit and then accept industry funds to promote a viewpoint that is in conflict with the vast majority of the worldwide scientific community?

Clearly, a conflict of interest such as this deserves immediate attention and a swift response. On behalf of the students at the University of Virginia and the questionable future that global warming holds for them, nothing short of his resignation will do.

Given the coal industry's deep pockets to continue funding lies while record heat waves sweep the country, I'm quite certain Michaels will have no problem finding a job within that industry.

Sincerely,
Laurie David

proudly framed and hung that report in our guest bathroom.

So there I am in Cincinnati, writing pithy lines about the Dodge Dart. Unbeknownst to me, the master plan begins to unfold. I stayed just long enough to actually produce a television spot. All of a sudden, I am in showbiz at a Dodge Dart dealership! Well, that one script gave me enough experience to get me a little closer to a better job with a magazine. That was my second lesson: every job doesn't have to be perfect—it just needs to move you a few inches forward. It will all make sense years later.

As an associate editor at *Tee-Shirt Weekly* (okay, it wasn't exactly *Rolling Stone*, but it *was* a magazine), most of my reporting was about cotton versus polyester, but there was also an opportunity to write articles about how rock-band merchandise was being ripped off by bootleggers. Pretty soon, I found myself interviewing music-industry veterans about rock-and-roll shirts and hats—*finally*, I was on the fringes of the entertainment industry! The little bit of music background helped me land my next job as a reporter for *Record World* magazine. The very next year, word was out that *Late Night with David Letterman* was looking for a researcher/music person—and jackpot!

Hanging around comedians was not bad for a day job, and when I left the show four years later, it was like I'd graduated from Comedy U. I started my own management company, representing comedians and developing sitcoms for television. My first client was comedian Chris Elliott, affectionately known then as "The Guy under the Stairs." I began producing my clients' stand-up specials. In fact, eventually, I married a comedian myself (see foreword).

My concerns about global warming began soon after we had our first child. I was a new mom, feeling very overwhelmed with the realization

Will God Still Bless America if We Despoil the Earth?

February 2, 2006
During his State of the Union speech, President Bush said: "Human life is a gift from our Creator—and that gift should never be *discarded, devalued, or put up for sale.*" [Emphasis added.] I am sure the president would agree that as stewards of creation, we have to care for all life on this planet and match our words with our deeds.

Mr. President, your policies are doing the opposite of what you declared so important last night. You are *discarding* the scientific conclusions of your NASA staff who have said that we have less than ten years to slow global warming before we are facing a "different planet." You are *devaluing* pristine wilderness by drilling in Alaska for a supply of oil that will do nothing to help break our addiction to oil. And you have *put up for sale* our planet's future by continuing to do nothing to slow carbon emissions.

Will God still bless America if her mountains are carved away, her prairies despoiled, her oceans polluted, and her climate forever altered? Please Mr. President, do your best to cherish and care for all of creation.

that I was now irreversibly responsible for this tiny creature. There was no turning back. I remember crying every day at five in the afternoon, the witching hour, my stress level at a breaking point. My husband and I would look at each other as if to say, "What have we done?"

I hated those first few months of motherhood. The baby had colic, Larry was on a soundstage seven days a week, my career was on hold—all of my friends worked—I had no one to talk to. I was isolated and scared. I spent a lot of time walking around the neighborhood, pushing a stroller. I started noticing an enormous amount of SUVs on the street. Everyone was driving them. I frequented a local bookstore and picked up a book called *High and Mighty* by Keith Bradsher of *The New York Times*. It was about the proliferation of SUVs and how they were really harming America. It explained that our fuel-economy standards were plunging because of a loophole in the law that classified SUVs as trucks, thereby allowing them to have lower mileage standards than regular cars—fewer miles per gallon and double the carbon-dioxide emissions. So, every time you drove somewhere, to the store, the school, the freeway, you were now all of a sudden doubling your personal CO_2 pollution. I panicked, because everyone I knew was driving them. I had had other lightbulb moments in my life—like the first time I tasted good wine and then couldn't drink the cheap stuff any more; or the moment that I learned that bald men make better lovers, and never dated a man with hair again. But this was different. This awareness landed with a thud on my shoulders. And with awareness comes responsibility.

Wangari Maathai is a woman who, with limited resources and living in Africa, spent thirty years inspiring the planting of 30 million trees across Kenya and spreading the

"I feel more at home in the sea than any other place on the planet. I want to help stop global warming because I want to protect my home. I want to be able to share the riches of my experiences with my daughters in the ocean. I want them to know her salty taste and powerful body. To have respect for the wonderment that is nature and weather. The only way I will be able to pass that on is if I get involved. I have been given the rides of a lifetime by the ocean. There is nothing more precious than our natural home. I want to take care of her. I know we can make a difference one by one."

—Laird Hamilton

message that protecting the environment protects democracy. For this, she became the first environmentalist ever to win the Nobel Peace Prize. She explained her lightbulb moment this way: "Passion begins with a burden and a split-second moment when you understand something like never before. That burden is on those who know. Those who don't know are at peace. Those of us who do know get disturbed and are forced to take action."

I often wonder what she was thinking when she planted those first few seeds in her backyard. Digging that first hole, was she wearing gloves or did she use her bare hands? Did she imagine that, ten years later, she would inspire a national movement? Did she know she was an activist?

Activism comes in all shapes, sizes, and at all ages. Looking back, I trace my very first action not on behalf of a cause but on behalf of a band. At the tender age of twelve, I was a huge Beatles fan, and when the film *Let It Be* was released, I was afraid that people might not go see it, as their popularity at that time was waning. So, I wanted to help. I remember cutting the movie ads out of the local newspaper, taking thumbtacks off of my bulletin board, and heading to the street, where I proceeded to tack the ad upon every telephone pole within a mile radius of my house. Surely, that would help get people into the theater!

The Civil Rights Movement of Our Time

After connecting the dots when I became a mom, I made it my job to educate myself about the environment and global warming. I read everything on the subject I could get my hands on: books and articles by reporter Mark Hertsgaard (*Earth Odyssey*); environmentalist Bill McKibben (*The End of Nature*); Pulitzer Prize–winning writer Ross Gelbspan (*Boiling Point*); Todd Wilkinson (*Science under Siege*); and Al Gore (*Earth in the Balance*). I joined the board of the Natural Resources Defense Council (NRDC), the most effective environmental group in the country. And through them, I met Robert F. Kennedy Jr., NRDC's senior attorney. Hearing him describe environmental problems as *the* civil rights issue of our time resonated so deeply with me that it was at that very moment that I decided to devote everything I had to the cause—to become a serious full-timer. Suddenly, developing sitcoms for television no longer felt so important. *Seinfeld* was a huge hit, and I certainly wasn't going to develop anything better than that. So, I began to hold regular salons in my house with policy makers, scientists, and experts on a wide range of environmental issues. I learned how to ask my friends for money to support the NRDC's work, and I quickly understood that if you educate yourself and care about these things, you can convince

> "College students have always led the charge on issues ranging from genocide in the Sudan to civil rights at home. Now, Stop Global Warming is asking them to take the lead on a problem of worldwide significance: the destruction of the planet. Whether it be wildfires in California or melting glaciers in Antarctica, mankind's impact on the environment is becoming more visible every day."
> —mtvU

others to care. I produced fund-raising events and raised millions of dollars. Ultimately, if you want to effect change, you have to get politically active too. So, I began supporting politicians who had good voting records on the environment, and before I handed a check over, I grilled them on the issues. And then the 2004 presidential election came.

I woke up the morning after the election, November 3, and cried for three straight days. I couldn't stop. Not because my candidate lost, which he had, but because of what it meant for the solutions to global warming. We had just reelected a president who surrounds himself with advisors and staff culled from the oil and auto industries, two giants fighting change at all costs. In fact, the president's first act in office in 2001 was to renege on his promise to regulate CO_2 as a pollutant. Two months later, he shocked the world by removing the United States from the Kyoto Protocol, an agreement that was the result of thousands of hours of work, endless meetings, difficult negotiations—basically blood,

---

Ticked Off in Seattle: A Tale of Two Washingtons

April 16, 2006

I just got back from Seattle, where I had the pleasure of spending some time with a global warming hero, Mayor Greg Nickels. He is proof positive that taking strong actions locally can have far-reaching impact. Last year, Nickels organized the U.S. Mayors' Climate Protection Agreement, which currently includes 224 mayors representing more than 44 million people in thirty-nine states.

Cities that endorse the agreement pledge to reduce their emissions and take other important steps to reduce their contribution to global warming. Seattle, for example, is transitioning its 3,000-vehicle fleet to hybrids and biofuels, and has already reduced city-government emissions by more than 60 percent since 1990. "I got ticked. I was embarrassed that our country didn't sign the Kyoto Protocol, so I committed to do something on behalf of the people of Seattle," Nickels told an audience.

Seven days earlier, I was on Capitol Hill in Washington, D.C., where it's easy to get depressed by the total lack of action by Congress and the White House.

Only 3,000 miles separates Seattle and the "other" Washington, yet on this all-important issue, they are light-years apart.

Hot and Windy in Dallas

April 19, 2006

How appropriate to be kicking off the Dallas premiere of *Too Hot NOT To Handle* in this unseasonable 101-degree Texas heat.

There is no stranger fish out of water than me at the Dallas airport. I know it sounds cliché, but I swear the guy sitting next to me on the plane turned on his computer and had a glam shot of a Hummer on his desktop.

The Lone Star State's power plants belched out more than 255 million tons of CO_2 last year, "leading" the nation in greenhouse gas pollution.

Doesn't Texas know that it could potentially generate more than 98 percent of its electricity from wind power? According to the West Texas Wind Energy Consortium, West Texas already supplies more than a quarter of the wind energy produced in the U.S. And there's more where that came from. Texas ranks second only to North Dakota in wind-energy potential (and first in solar potential), but it needs some encouragement. Texas could be a renewable powerhouse, perhaps supplying up to a third of the total U.S. demand with its renewable resources. All it takes is a little political leadership.

sweat, and tears—on the part of 160 countries, including the United States.

On day four of my crying jag, I finally pulled myself together and called three people: John Adams, NRDC's founder; Frances Bienecke, the group's president; and Bobby Kennedy—my three guides and mentors. I pitched to them an idea of how I thought we could—*had to*—build a huge grassroots movement demanding solutions to global warming. A giant march on Washington to stop global warming, but on the Internet instead of on the streets. A virtual march that would continue every day until we were millions strong, combining all of our voices into one loud, clear cry for action. Frances said, "Fantastic." John said, "Great, we are in." Bobby said, "I don't get it. What do you mean *virtual*?" And, believe me, that was the hardest thing I did that year, explaining to a guy who has never touched a computer what the heck *virtual* meant. Eventually, he was in too, along with dozens of other organizations and environmental groups, including the Sierra Club, Union of Concerned Scientists, Care2, The Conservation Fund,

National Wildlife Federation, National Council of Churches, the Indy Racing League, Tides Network, Roots, myspace.com, and dozens more.

The next step was to find a prominent Republican to help launch the Virtual March, because, as we all know, this issue is not political, it is moral. If global warming became associated with just one political party, we would never get to where we need to go. The obvious first stop was John McCain, who has been a long-time outspoken leader on global warming. And I have to say that it was my stature as an NRDC trustee that got me into his Senate office. (Okay, maybe he was a *Curb Your Enthusiasm* fan, too, and *Seinfeld*, well, that certainly didn't hurt—I am the first to use the proverbial "wife of" when needed. Another life lesson: use what you've got.) But still, he knew I had the support of the most powerful and respected environmental group in the world, and that goes a long way when you are knocking on doors in Washington. In his office, on the spot, he said to me, "Let's get marching."

Large numbers of people can change the world. Look at what we have accomplished before. In 1963, the March on Washington changed the debate on civil rights when people poured into the streets to demand action. In 1970, millions turned out for the first Earth Day, which led directly to the establishment of the Clean Air Act and Endangered Species Act, not to mention the formation of the Environmental Protection Agency. (We have to give Nixon credit for that. It is truly ironic that the early days of the environmental movement were actually spurred on by the Republican Party, Teddy Roosevelt being an obvious example. Unfortunately, the Republican Party has truly been absent on these issues in recent years. We need all Republicans back in this movement, now.) Large numbers of people did that. And we can do it again. We have to do it again. And now we have even better tools; now we have the Internet. New tactics for a new day.

The Stop Global Warming Virtual March has three basic goals: to get Americans to admit that the globe is warming;

to acknowledge that we are causing it; and to demand from our government and business community meaningful solutions. So that's one important yet easy thing you can all do *today*, and it only requires an e-mail address. Join the Virtual March and think of ways to get others to join, too. Spreading the word is building the movement. Who knows better than you what it takes to engage your personal sphere of friends, associates, teachers, and family? If everyone signs on and sends it to five friends, we can become so big and so strong that Congress and the Administration will no longer be able to ignore this problem. Go to www.stopglobalwarming.org and add your voice to the two NFL teams, religious leaders, politicians, Jon Bon Jovi, James Taylor, Incubus, surfer Laird Hamilton, Senator Hillary Clinton, skateboarder Tony Hawk, Governor Arnold Schwarzenegger, Leonardo DiCaprio, Senator Barack Obama, MTV, myspace.com, the National Council of Churches, The Weather Channel, and almost half a million Americans who are already virtually marching. One voice can turn into a million, and a million voices will be heard!

Once the Virtual March was launched, I started to focus my efforts on other projects to get the issue into popular culture. First were two television projects: *Earth to America!*, featuring today's top comedians, including Will Ferrell, Tom Hanks, Steve Martin, Jack Black, Larry David, Martin Short, Robin Williams, and Ray Romano, using comedy as a way to get the word out about global warming; and a one-hour documentary film I produced for HBO called *Too Hot NOT To Handle*, which focused on the effects of global warming in the United States. (It premiered on April 22, 2006).

And the third part of the plan was a feature film. The story behind *An Inconvenient Truth* is a Hollywood tale in and of itself. I was asked to moderate a town-hall meeting on global warming in New York City on Thursday, May 27, 2004, to coincide with the opening of the Hollywood blockbuster *The Day after Tomorrow*. Al Gore was one of several panelists and he showed a ten-minute version of his now-famous hour-long slide show. I had never seen it before, and I was floored. As soon as the evening's program concluded, I asked him to let me present his full briefing to leaders and friends in New York and Los Angeles. I would do all the organizing if he would commit to the dates. Gore's presentation was the most powerful and clear explanation of global warming I had ever seen. And it became my mission to get everyone I knew to see it too. I firmly believed that if George Bush himself saw it, he would be moved to start solving the problem immediately. In Los Angeles, I rented a hotel ballroom, printed invitations, and hit the phones. In New York, the Society for Ethical Culture donated their venue, Ken Sunshine Consultants donated their public-relations help, and prominent New Yorkers cohosted the evening. Bobby Kennedy convinced Roger Ailes, president of Fox News, to attend. We met with Roger the following week, and in the room he committed to a one-hour primetime news special on global warming. This was a huge accomplishment, for obvious reasons. Fox News would be a new messenger, and although everyone urged us not to work with Fox, telling us the network would never do a "fair and balanced" show, Fox surprised everyone with *The Heat Is On.* (Unfortunately, six months later, in an apparent caving to advertisers—perhaps car companies? ExxonMobile?—Fox News ran a second piece, ostensibly to give "opposing views" a chance to rebut. This was a sad step backward and a major disservice to its viewers.) On both coasts the packed houses, although some were initially cynical, all gave Gore a standing ovation.

At this point, Gore was logging thousands of air miles crisscrossing the world, literally our modern-day Paul Revere. But a filmed version could reach millions—and quickly. And that is what we did.

Helping to bring Al Gore's keynote on global warming to a "theater near you" has been the highlight of my career.

Environmentalist Is Not a Four-Letter Word

Although it is becoming more and more obvious to people that environmentalism is something we must all embrace, it has taken some courage over the last decade for Americans to do so. Clever self-interests have successfully scared people away from the fight by insisting that to be an environmentalist, you must be held to a gold standard of perfection. Environmentalists even do it to each other. Unless you live in a solar-powered house, are a practicing vegan, wear hemp clothes, and bike to work, no need to apply here. These qualifications would scare away pretty much everyone I know, and I know a lot of environmentalists. I've been asked, "Do you eat meat?" The not-so-subtle subtext being, well, if you do, you aren't really an environmentalist. I've been asked, "What are your shoes made of?" The subtext being that if they're leather, well, you're just a hypocrite.

> "The longer we wait, the more difficult it will be to mitigate the effects of climate change. Are we going to hand our children and grandchildren a world vastly different from the one that we now inhabit?"
>
> —Senator John McCain

A criticism that follows me is that I "jet-set across the country in my own fleet of private planes." Well, for the record, I don't own a plane, and the great majority of my air travel is commercial. I have the frequent-flier miles to prove it. But critics want nothing more than to marginalize your ability to affect change, to weaken your message. There is plenty to criticize in my lifestyle—believe me, I don't need help from others, I am my own worst critic—but I try to do the best I can and to give back more than I take. That's what

I work on—setting my own standard for myself.

Sir David King, Tony Blair's top science advisor, complained bitterly that funded "skeptics" were showing up at all of his speaking engagements and disrupting them in an attempt to intimidate him and weaken his message. That accusation, from one of the world's most esteemed scientists, helped expose the organized efforts of ExxonMobil and others to purposely confuse the public. *Mother Jones* magazine exposed in detail the millions that the oil company has been spending on "think tanks" to create doubt about global warming.

The vilification of environmentalists picked up steam during the 1970s via the spokesmen for polluting industries in response to the great progress we were making with federal environmental legislation. The practice of mocking environmentalism was amplified by President Ronald Reagan, who during the 1980 election declared, "I am a Sagebrush Rebel," a reference to his solidarity with the extremist "wise-use" coalition made up of corporate polluters such as beer baron Joseph Coors and a cadre of Western ranchers, miners, and developers who helped launch his presidency. While serving as governor of California, Reagan had made his disdain for environmental conservation clear, claiming at one point during the battle to

---

Saluting a Global Warming Hero

April 6, 2006

I recently attended the Nation Institute's Ridenhour Awards for Truth Telling to help honor Rick Piltz. Piltz is the former NASA employee who resigned in protest after Philip Cooney, the former oil industry hack, altered and significantly weakened the meaning of an arduously researched global warming report Piltz had prepared.

When the story hit the press, Cooney was shown the White House door—then, in one of the quickest turnarounds in job-seeking history, was hired two days later by ExxonMobil.

By sacrificing his job, Piltz shined a bright light on the administration's epidemic disregard for science. So it was a thrill to see him being recognized for his courage—and for showing Americans that misinformation can come from the very places designed to protect them.

You Can't Make This Stuff Up

September 28, 2005
This morning, the Senate's Environment and Public Works Committee will hit an all-time low when it comes to wasting taxpayer time and money by calling in science fiction writer Michael Crichton to testify on global warming. I kid you not.

Crichton's latest novel alleges that environmentalists created global warming to make it easier to collect fundraising dollars. At a time when we cannot afford to waste another minute in protecting the American people against continued extreme weather events, having Crichton testify is an unbelievable misuse of public resources.

Perhaps Sen. Jim Inhofe (R-OK), chairman of the aforementioned committee, should call Stephen King as his next witness, because if the Senator's global warming–denying viewpoint prevails, our future will surely be a horrific nightmare.

protect the state's dwindling old-growth forests from clear-cutting, "A tree is a tree, how many more do you need to look at?" When asked about his visit to one of the oldest stands of redwoods, Reagan said, "I saw them; there is nothing beautiful about them, just that they are a little higher than the others."

Disparaging environmentalists reached an all-time high during the 1992 election when then–President George H. W. Bush derisively labeled Al Gore "Ozone Man" and said, "This guy is so far out in the environmental extreme, we'll be up to our necks in owls and outta work for every American." You can see him make the statement yourself in *An Inconvenient Truth*. George W. Bush continued the legacy in the 2000 campaign when he cracked that Gore "likes electric cars. He just doesn't like making electricity." In retrospect, the mocking now seems so vicious and transparent, and the efforts of polluters to paint people who care about the Earth as wackos so dated. Being anti-environmentalist is as absurd as being anti-children.

Why all the nasty name-calling? Money, money, money. Certain industries are going to have to change, and it's going to cost them something to do it, so they are resisting at all costs. The day *An Inconvenient Truth* opened, an ExxonMobil front organization called the Competitive Enterprise Institute released pathetic ads extolling the virtues of all things carbon dioxide. The last line of the commercial says, "They call it pollution, we call it life." I swear, I didn't make that up. It was a desperate attempt to try and discredit Gore, the film, and the environmental community as a whole. It didn't work. The auto industry, in a potentially planet-destroying move, convinced everyone through a multimillion-dollar ad campaign that driving an SUV was the safest car you could put your children into, when over time the opposite has been proven true. Of course, it is in the auto industry's best interests to keep these cars on the road, as they earn more than $10,000 in pure profit for each SUV sold. Now we are stuck with a car of choice that gets an average of six miles per gallon less than a regular vehicle (which aren't so great either) and is the heaviest we've had in three decades. President Jimmy Carter increased our fuel economy only to have it reversed again by Ronald Reagan. And you all know the tobacco industry's legacy of lies—same tactics, different product.

The point is, we have to start questioning the messen-

Does the President Think Global Warming Will Be Good for the Economy?

July 11, 2005

Last week at the G8, President Bush restated his favorite global warming canard: that mandatory curbs on fossil-fuel pollution will "cripple the U.S. economy." *Well, what does he think global warming will do to the economy?!*

Nonstop flooding, killer heat waves, energy and food shortages—what will these do to the economy? Will it be good for Wall Street when millions of people are displaced from coastal cities? Come to think of it, isn't Wall Street about five blocks from the Atlantic Ocean? How are all those brokers going to feel about relocating to Wichita?

Bush's other favorite strategy for evading responsibility on global warming is the popular third-grade school-yard chant "I know you are, but what am I?" According to Bush, we aren't going to do anything about greenhouse emissions if China and India don't do it too.

But we are responsible right now for more global warming pollution than either country. And, by the way, you can't even sell many American cars in China because they don't meet that country's higher fuel standards. That's right, China demands better mileage from its cars than we do!

ger. Who is saying it and why are they saying it? Who is funding them and why? You know all those global warming "skeptics" you keep hearing about? Well, if someone pays you to be skeptical, I suppose that is what you will be, regardless of the facts, if you are also lacking a conscience.

The bright side is that it is a sure sign that you're making an impact when the opposition starts attacking. Second only to female country singers, Hollywood celebrities take the most heat for speaking out. Bruce Springsteen, who regularly speaks his mind during his sold-out concerts, was asked recently by CNN if he worries about alienating his audience by voicing his political opinions. Springsteen said, "You are saying musicians shouldn't speak up? ... You know ... it's insane ... You know ... it's funny ... That's called common sense." And he went on to ask why is it okay for right-wing ideologues with no particular qualifications to espouse their opinions night and day on radio and TV but not a musician or an artist? Good point, Bruce.

> "It drives me crazy to see so much of this planet's life so casually endangered. The first steps are so easy (drive smaller cars, for instance) that it's very hard to understand why we haven't taken them. But I know that this is the issue our generation will be judged by."
> · —Bill McKibben

We need to get our values straight and applaud anyone who risks his or her personal cachet to make a difference. Shining a light on an issue is one big way of giving back and should be admired and encouraged. Free speech ultimately rules, and despite the risk of box-office backlash, right-wing ridicule, or record sale drops, citizens (celebrities are citizens too) such as George Clooney, Neil Young, Bono, the Dixie Chicks, Angelina Jolie, Leonardo DiCaprio, Brad Whitford, Ted Danson, Mary Steenburgen, Faith Hill, Rob Reiner, Tim McGraw, and many others have used their personal clout to speak out on substantive issues. That is true patriotism.

If I have learned anything from my activism, it is this: we are all guilty and we all have to be part of the solution. We have to do the best we can and then try to do better. It's not about any one person doing everything; it's about all of us doing something and then maybe a little more. Country singer Tim McGraw put it best when he said, "It's not about sacrifice, it's about change."

What You Can Do

How much time do you have? Do you want to do a little bit or a lot? Start locally and build. Start small and grow. Start in your house, then move to your school, your book club, your gym, your church, your temple, your city. Start with your friends and family. Reach out to people who don't agree with you. Talk to that relative you always fight with at Thanksgiving dinner. (In my house, we barely make it past the soup course before the debates begin.)

Activism can be as simple as forwarding an important article to those on your e-mail list. Just because something is printed in the newspaper doesn't mean anyone sees it. Often, really critical articles are buried inside the paper. (An important article confirming the links of global warming to the ferocity of hurricanes was printed in *The New York Times* on the bottom of page 16.) If you forward an article to ten people and then they forward it to their ten friends, the next thing you know, you have seriously helped to get the word out and influenced public opinion along the way. The Internet is our greatest new weapon. Stephen Colbert's now famous appearance at a White House correspondents' dinner was seen by 2,700 people in the room that night, but by millions more on the Internet.

Make small changes in your apartment, house, and lifestyle. Bring your own reusable cup to Starbucks. Choose a hybrid car, wear a Stop Global Warming bracelet, send DVDs of HBO's *Too Hot NOT to Handle* and *An Inconvenient Truth* as Christmas gifts. Donate the DVDs to a school after you watch them. Sponsor your child's class on a field trip to a movie theater to see films such as *An Inconvenient Truth*. I know several science teachers who assigned watching the trailer on the Internet as homework. Get involved, and join a local or national environmental group (for example, membership to the Natural Resources Defense Council costs $15). When their numbers swell, their power as lobbyists in Washington grows too. Read the newsletters these groups send you, then pass them on. Buy memberships for your teachers as gifts. If you can't do the work, support the groups that do.

Pull chargers from the wall and turn computers off (wasted energy use is 10 percent of your energy bill). If your cell phone, iPod, or digital camera is unplugged from the charger, but the charger is still in the wall, it is draining energy. Turning on a light switch uses energy that is likely made in a way that causes global warming pollution, so turn the lights off when you leave the room. Teach your kids to do it too. Install light sensors whenever you can, especially in office buildings. On vacation or a business trip, tell the hotel manager to lower the air-conditioning, offer guests the option to reuse towels and sheets, and suggest light timers for their rooms. There is now a better lightbulb, compact fluorescent (CFL), and it works like a charm—it uses 66 percent less energy than a regular lightbulb and can last up to fifteen times longer. If every household changed from using five regular lightbulbs to the compact fluorescents, it would be the equivalent of taking 8 million cars off the road for a year.

> "Global warming is a matter of national security. Will we live in a world where we must fight our neighbors for fresh water and food? Or will we take the lead now and leave to our children and grandchildren a world better off than the one we inherited from our parents? Shoulder-to-shoulder, let's march together to save what God loaned us, so our children and their children will live in a world we would recognize a hundred years from now. No excuses. No apologies. Take the first step today. We can't do it without you."
> —General Wesley Clark

Bring a garment bag to the dry cleaners so your clothes don't have to be wrapped in all that plastic and paper. Return

Comfort versus Conscience—The Bathroom Battle Has Begun!

May 19, 2005

I recently saw a very disturbing presentation about the paper industry, which is the third-largest contributor to global warming pollution. Apparently, Kimberly-Clark—the world's largest tissue-paper producer, and the maker of that box of Kleenex sitting on your nightstand—is also a leading destroyer of virgin forests.

Well, action starts at home, so I immediately replaced all of our toilet paper and tissues with post-consumer recycled materials. I did this quietly and anonymously. I wanted to see who in my family would complain first. It didn't take long for my daughter to register her objections. She has since taken to carrying a rather large backpack with her at all times—ostensibly to handle her volumes of homework, but really to hoard softer brands from all the bathrooms she visits on play dates. The next complaint came quite surprisingly in the middle of a lecture series my husband and I were attending. Larry looked at me and screamed, "I can't sit here anymore because of your damn new toilet paper!"

all those extra hangers. Buy in bulk. Buy appliances that have an Energy Star label—this signifies the most energy-efficient brand, and the difference between these and the less-efficient ones is enormous. For instance, if you buy one of today's most energy-efficient refrigerators, it will use less than half the energy of a model that's twelve years old or older. Defrost your freezer. When ice builds up, it actually requires more energy to keep it cold. Only run your dishwasher if it's full. Don't prerinse dishes. Don't preheat ovens. Don't overdry your towels and clothes. Hang things to dry when you can. Clean vents and change filters. (When your dryer filter is clogged, it needs more energy to run.) Conserve, reduce, reuse, recycle.

Think. Think about where things come from, how they get made, where they end up when thrown away. Let's start with something basic, such as toilet paper, an item found in every home in America, that is still made today mostly from virgin trees cut down from rare 100- or 150-year-old trees in northern Canada. A virgin tree is from a forest untouched by man. Trees, which absorb carbon dioxide, can't do the job if they're cut. Is it really necessary to destroy endangered forests for toilet paper, tissues, and paper towels? If every household in the United States replaced just one roll of virgin toilet paper with one recycled postconsumer waste roll, 424,000 trees would still be standing. Kleenex (facial tissue), Puffs (facial tissue), Bounty (paper towels), Scott (paper towels), Viva (paper towels), Cottonelle (toilet paper), and Charmin (toilet paper) are all still made from virgin trees, some of which come from virgin forests. Did you know that? Will you make a different choice now that you do know? Would these companies make a different choice if they knew their customers refused to buy them?

Pass your magazines on to a friend, hospital, library, or nursing home. Make your office recycle and buy paper products that are made from postconsumer waste. The paper industry is the third-largest contributor to global warming pollution. If every household in the United States bought recycled napkins instead of virgin fiber napkins, we would save a million trees.

What about plastic bags? Americans throw away about *100 billion* plastic bags a year; less than 1 percent of these are recycled. Plastic bags come from petroleum, and the manufacturing of just fourteen of those plastic bags uses the same amount of oil that it would take to drive a car one mile. Paper bags are even worse. Producing paper bags uses four times the energy as making plastic ones, as reported by the Environmental Protection Agency. And right now, only about 20 percent of the paper bags in use are recycled. And most of that plastic and paper ends up in landfills, which—you guessed it—emit global warming pollution.

> "We all take advantage of the great natural resources the Earth gives us and we have no desire to see its shores and communities flooded. Get involved and take an active interest by getting educated! One person working diligently alone can do wonders, but many people working harmoniously together can accomplish worlds."
>
> —Incubus

Recycle your newspaper. Sixty-three million newspapers

are printed each day in the United States; 44 million of these will be thrown away. American businesses throw away 21 million tons of paper every year. That comes to about 175 pounds per office worker. Cut that in half by printing on both sides.

Catalog retailers mail out about 17 billion catalogs every year—that's nearly sixty per person in the United States (most of which go from the mailbox directly to the trash can)—and almost none of them use postconsumer recycled-content paper. Call the companies and get your name off their mailing lists. By printing its catalogs on 10 percent postconsumer recycled paper (and aiming for 30 percent by 2008), Norm Thompson's industry-leading effort has saved 4,400 tons of wood per year, 20 billion BTUs (British Thermal Units) of energy, and 11.7 million gallons of water.

Start a mug movement in your office. We throw away some 25 billion polystyrene cups every year, most of which end up in landfills too. Our habits have gotten so bad that we grab an individual water bottle every time we are thirsty, even when we are in our homes. Whatever happened to filling a glass? Where do all those water bottles go? Americans buy about 25 billion single-serve plastic water bottles each year, according to the Container Recycling Institute. More than 80 percent of these bottles are thrown away or become litter. Buried in a landfill, a plastic bottle can take up to 1,000 years to biodegrade. According to the Earth Policy Institute, the plastic used to satisfy Americans' demand for bottled water requires more than 1.5 million barrels of oil annually, enough to fuel 100,000 U.S. cars for a year. Worldwide, some 2.7 million tons of plastic are used to bottle water each year. We have an entire generation of kids who are growing up thinking that the only way to drink water is from an individual plastic bottle. As the permanent weekly soccer-snack mom, I bought twenty reusable plastic cups for the kids to use on water breaks. Moms rotate taking them home to clean. We are still using them three years later. Throwing

away twenty or more dispos-
able cups a week for three
years would've wasted more
than 3,000 cups.

Get your office to
employ reusable coffee filters
(metal mesh or unbleached
cloth) instead of paper ones,
and use organically grown
coffee. White-paper coffee
filters bleached with chlorine
are not only bad for the environment (the paper mills
that bleach the filters dump
wastewater containing dioxins into waterways), but some
of the chlorine and dioxins
can end up in your coffee.

Plant trees and stop
using leaf blowers. (Rakes
work fine, and gas-powered
leaf blowers can generate as
much emissions in one hour
as driving a car 350 miles.)
Buy an electric mower; gas
mowers are among the dirtiest of our modern machines.
Ask your local gas station
when they will carry flex fuel
or biodiesel. Be a nudge,
keep asking.

Support organic and local
farmers—the Worldwatch
Institute estimates that the
ingredients for the average
American meal travel more than 1,500 miles from farm to fork!

Below the Belt— New Industry Ads Use Kids to Pimp Coal

May 5, 2006

This is as low as it gets, lower than any industry has gone to promote their product since Big Tobacco paid doctors to recommend certain brands of cigarettes. The coal industry's new ad campaign features a series of kids extolling the wonderful virtues of this dirtiest of fuels.

No matter how many cute kids they hire to pimp coal as nifty and clean, coal-burning power plants still pump out 40 percent of America's global warming CO_2 pollution, more than any other source.

Given our climate crisis, it's inexcusable for any industry not to be using available technologies to reduce their impact on the planet. Every penny they spend on advertising and lobbying to delay implementing near-term technological fixes is a penny not spent on real solutions.

So coal industry, how about it? Stop prostituting children in the name of your short-term greed. Dust off those promising technologies and implement them now, not in fifteen years or when the government finally gets around to forcing you to. Use your soaring profits to clean up your own act. That's the responsible thing to do—even one of your coal-ad kids could tell you that.

Sign up your classmates for the Virtual March. Compete with friends to see who can sign up the most students. Sit outside of a grocery store with a friend and a clipboard, signing people up. If they sign up, they will start getting informed. Information is power. Once you understand something, you can't go backward. You can't put the toothpaste back into the tube. Add a Stop Global Warming banner and link to your personal Web site. Start a blog. Talk about global warming on it. Read the blogs on Huffington post.com, and post responses. Be a regular caller to radio shows. Raise your voice. Be a squeaky wheel.

Get mad. Write letters to your local newspapers. Run for local offices—start small and climb the ladder. Every position is important, including those on school boards, town and county boards, and library boards, as well as parks and recreation commissioner, auditor, treasurer, and planning and zoning councils. Apply all you know to everything you do.

Start a no-idling rule at your school carpool lane. Ten percent of all our fuel use is wasted in idling. The myth that it uses more gas to turn your car on and off is just that—a myth. After only ten seconds, you use less gas to turn the ignition off. Parents and caregivers are often lined up for carpools anywhere from five to twenty minutes. Crossroads school in Los Angeles posted a no-idle sign in its carpool lane and it has made a huge difference.

Some book publishers have been leading the effort for several years to minimize the impact on virgin forests by printing books on recycled paper. In fact, the book you are holding in your hands right now is printed on 100 percent postconsumer recycled paper, using bio-energy for production.

By printing the first edition (2003) of *Harry Potter and the Order of the Phoenix* on 100 percent postconsumer recycled paper, Raincoast Books realized the following ecological savings: 39,320 trees saved, 63,435,801 liters of water saved (enough water to fill forty-two Olympic-sized swimming pools), 854,988 kilograms of solid waste avoided (equivalent to the weight of 209 average female elephants), 27,329 million BTUs of energy saved (enough electricity to power the average North American home for 262 years), and 1,645,243 kilograms of greenhouse gases avoided (equal to 5.3 million kilometers traveled by a car with average fuel efficiency).

Leading U.S. publisher Random House recently announced that by 2010, at least 30 percent of the uncoated paper it uses to print its books will have recycled paper content. Random House estimates that its shift to recycled paper by 2010 will save more than 550,000 trees per year (80,000 tons of wood), reduce greenhouse gas emissions by more than 88 million tons, and save 425 billion BTUs of energy.

Colleges are really stepping up and making serious changes on their campuses. Get yours to do it too. The University of Texas at El Paso has put all its air-conditioners on efficiency timers and expects to save at least $173,000 a year. The University of Florida at Gainesville has made it a mandate that all

Green Is the New Red, White, and Blue

March 3, 2006

Scientists, traditionally the world's most cautious human beings, are now saying we have less than ten years before we reach the point of no return on slowing global warming. Tony Blair has said seven. (And, since we are making predictions, I say five.)

Thankfully, we had a number of effective voices being raised on the issue this week, led by Barack Obama and New York Times columnist Tom Friedman (who coined the catchphrase for 2006: "Green is the new red, white, and blue").

Speaking to a gathering of the nation's governors, Obama called our leaders' efforts to reduce America's dependence on oil a "trance of inaction," pointing out: "President Bush's funding for renewable fuels is at the same level it was the day he took office."

For months now, Tom Friedman has been saying that the only solution to breaking our dependence on oil is to raise the gasoline tax. As Friedman points out, the public came to this conclusion without a single Democrat or Republican taking the lead on the gas tax issue.

As Andy Stern has said on this very site, leadership means going first. In the case of our administration, I would be happy to settle for them going second.

new cars purchased for the school fleet be hybrid or fuel-efficient equivalent. (Wouldn't that be a good idea for the United States government's fleet of more than 620,000 cars as well?) The University of Georgia is converting their fleet—the largest in the country for a university—to biofuels. The University of Miami offers a 50 percent parking discount for hybrid cars. Students and faculty are all eligible, and the savings can be as high as $325 per year.

Pay attention to the efforts of companies doing good things and support them. If you own stocks in public companies (or plan to), become active in developing shareholder resolutions, and vote your shares to move companies in the right direction. Companies do listen to these criticisms from their shareholders, even before they gain majority support. Knowing that a shareholder resolution asking the company to deal with computer waste was coming to the table, Apple Computer announced two weeks before its annual meeting that it was instituting a full recycling program for all new Mac buyers, marking a huge success before the fight ever really started. Choose products with the least packaging and complain to companies that overpackage items.

> "I am marching because of my love of the outdoors. Growing up in the Pacific Northwest, I was instilled with a sense of pride for all of the beauty and fun that the outdoors gave to me. I spent my time playing in the forests of my hometown, fishing and crabbing at my grandfather's house on the Puget Sound, and going up to the mountains to play in the snow. My hope is that my son will be able to enjoy the same simple pleasures that I was able to enjoy as a child and still enjoy as an adult."
>
> —Cameron Cleeland

Reuse everything—take paper clips off of letters you receive and reuse them; reuse envelopes and write on the front *This envelope is being used again.* Print and copy on both sides of paper. Hollywood talent agency Endeavor sends most of its movie scripts by e-mail; any hard copies it ships are printed double sided, which saves about 12 million pieces of paper per year, and all scripts are recycled after use.

Growing numbers of companies have found that implementing changes that are good for the environment makes good business sense as well. By reducing the paper weight of its ATM receipts from twenty pounds to fifteen pounds, Bank of America not only saved paper, but saved $500,000 in annual expenses in transportation, storage, and handling. Since 2003, by recycling and buying recycled paper, the Eagles football team has saved nearly 90 tons of wood from virgin forests, kept 139 metric tons of greenhouse gases out of the atmosphere, and saved 5.46 billion BTUs of energy. DuPont cut its greenhouse gas emissions by 72 percent by 2003, and reaped large financial benefits from their leaner operations, saving a whopping $3 billion through energy conservation.

> "Global warming is one of the most serious environmental and economic threats of our generation. Failure to act is not an option. That is why, along with seven other state attorneys general from around the country, I filed a pioneering lawsuit requiring the nation's dirtiest coal-fired power plants to slash their carbon pollution. I commend every citizen who has become informed and involved in the global warming issue."
>
> —Attorney General Eliot Spitzer

Suggest to your bosses or employees incentives for carpoolers and hybrid-car drivers. Offer premium parking spaces or early happy-hour Fridays for employees who increase their carpool hours. Bank of America offers its employees a cash rebate of $3,000 for a new hybrid purchase. Google employees get a $5,000 rebate for buying hybrid cars. What changes can you set in motion at your office or school?

Calculate your own carbon footprint at stopglobal warming.org or climatecrisis.net. Your estimated annual CO_2 footprint is the total CO_2 produced by your daily lifestyle. You can offset your personal or business carbon emissions by supporting organizations that build new wind farms, plant trees, and develop solar energy.

Everyone is offsetting these days. Dave Matthews Band has made donations to green causes to offset all of the carbon dioxide caused by air travel and energy use from their tours going back to 1991. When Coldplay cut *A Rush of Blood to the Head*, the band decided to buy 10,000 mango trees for villagers in Karnataka, India. Because the trees breathe CO_2 as they grow, Coldplay figures the mango trees will eventually neutralize all the CO_2 released in the making and selling of its CDs. In Manchester, Tennessee, the Bonnaroo Music Festival offset all of the carbon emissions produced by the festival by purchasing Cool Tag wind credits. The World Cup was carbon neutral in 2006 for the first time ever. The Fédération Internationale de Football Association offset 100,000 tons of carbon dioxide linked to the construction and maintenance of the twelve stadiums and the travel and accommodation of the 3.2 million spectators. The organizers plan to spend part of the funds to replace coal-fired boilers at a South African factory with boilers that can run on sawdust, and also by planting trees in India and South Africa to soak up CO_2.

Only support politicians who will do something to reduce our country's emissions. Campaign for them, hold them accountable. Flood your local representatives with calls and e-mails. Campaign for good environmental candidates.

Voluntary Measures Don't Work: Why We Need 45 mpg Cars Now

October 3, 2005

Okay, so how many of you drove a little less and a little slower this week in response to President Bush's helpful hints on saving gas? That's what I thought. So much for voluntary measures. They just don't work—just like they didn't work when the president asked power-plant operators to voluntarily reduce their carbon emissions.

George Bush's halfhearted attempt to persuade Americans to reduce fuel consumption is about as believable as those new ads from ExxonMobile and Chevron telling us "Slow down ... Save gas." The sincerity practically leaps off the page. The Bush White House and the oil companies have always been in synch—but asking us to slow down by ten mph is the best they can come up with? Thanks for the suggestion, guys! How about raising the mpg our cars have to get by ten miles per gallon instead? It would reduce our crushing dependence on oil a heck of a lot faster than requesting we ease off the accelerator a bit.

Check their environmental ratings through the League of Conservation Voters, which tracks how every member of Congress votes on each environmental issue. For example, you could quickly identify an anti-planet candidate such as Representative Richard Pombo (R-CA, 11th), whose score has never reached double digits in his seven terms (Pombo scored a zero in 2004, a three for the 108th Congress, 2003–2004. Boy, you have to really make an effort to score that low) or a politician with a proven track record of protecting the environment, such as Representative George Miller (D-CA, 7th), who had a perfect 100 score in 2005. Find out if your mayor is part of the U.S. Mayors Climate Protection Agreement. If not, get a few friends together and schedule a meeting. Go to his or her office, show up. They work for you.

> "America needs to be a leader in the fight to stem the pace of increase in global average temperature, by coming up with a national energy policy, something we currently lack."
> —Governor Brian Schweitzer

Every day, someone tells me a great new idea. My friend Bonnie Berger suggested that each state should sell a Stop Global Warming license plate, the ultimate vanity plate, with funds going to local global warming education. A popular exercise instructor in L.A. offered a free class in exchange for a ticket stub from *An Inconvenient Truth*. A woman whose grandmother passed away asked, in lieu of flowers, that donations be made to stopglobalwarming.org.

Kenny Luna, an eighth-grade science teacher in Babylon, New York, came up with the challenge to give one CFL bulb to every K–12 student in America. Home Depot agreed to supply Luna with enough CFL bulbs for every student in his district. Luna is now working to get other teachers across the country to join this effort.

My friend Lisa Foster took a sabbatical from teaching and went to Australia with her husband while he was shooting a movie. At the grocery store, she was impressed with the question the checker asked her: "Paper or reusable bag?" For most Australians, the only answer is the 99 cent eco bag that was sitting right there at the counter. When she returned to L.A., she quit her job and started a business selling her version of the all-purpose reusable bag. Although everyone told her the idea would never work here because Americans just don't care, in the first six months, she sold more than 20,000 to independent grocery stores around the country. Ask your local store manager if they will carry them.

Start with one thing and convince one other person to do it too. Let the domino effect begin. You get an idea, you influence another, and the next thing you know, we are all part of the biggest revolution this country has ever seen—a clean, efficient industrial revolution! Nothing short of that will do.

Stossel's "Myths" May Be on the Best-Seller List, but They Don't Belong on ABC

July 19, 2006

For some reason, John Stossel is often referred to as a journalist. In reality, he's a contrarian blowhard who believes that government is evil and that corporations would be the most ethical, noble institutions in the world if only they were left to their own devices and not hampered by pesky burdens like accountability and oversight. Riiight.

So it comes as little surprise to me that Stossel belittles the serious threat from global warming. Last week, he went on Fox News's *Dayside* to promote his new book, *Myths, Lies, and Downright Stupidity: Get out the Shovel—Why Everything You Know Is Wrong* (no sign of arrogance in that title …).

So what did "Mr. Mythbuster" have to say about global warming?

Stossel: "Global warming is happening. Is it a big problem? Probably not. Many scientists do not agree, despite what you hear in the Al Gore movie. And Kyoto wouldn't make any difference even if we did sign and if the countries that did obeyed, which they're not."

And there's more "downright stupidity." Stossel recently told Fox News's Bill O'Reilly that "we shouldn't wreck life for poor people" by trying to solve global warming through efforts like the Kyoto Protocol. (Huh? Poor people will suffer the worst from global warming.) Stossel admits there's been warming but thinks we need to wait for more evidence before we do anything about it. (Perhaps evidence such as the deadly heat wave now scorching the U.S. and straining our electric grid?)

Myths, Lies, and Downright Stupidity is really the perfect description of Stossel's reporting credentials. He's got a right-wing fan club, so ABC let him off easy for lying, then promoted him when Barbara Walters left *20/20*. Now, he's not only a "correspondent," he's an "anchor," granted the same prestige as Walters and other respectable network journos. "Give me a break!" would be the understatement of the decade there.

Nothing is a bigger myth or lie than this guy.

The Solution Is You!

Ten years ago, when I was first becoming aware that there were other things to be concerned about besides my career, my house, and my immediate world, I realized that I could do more and that I should do more. I know people always say that things aren't black-and-white, but I don't agree. Some things are just right or wrong. Motherhood taught me how to be a better nurturer, and once that happened, protecting the things that enrich our lives, things that once gone would never return, became of monumental importance to me. My activism, which was always inside me, took over. What do you mean we are cutting off the tops of mountains and dropping the debris into clean rivers and streams? What do you mean a corporation is going to destroy the last untouched breeding ground of the gray whale? What do you mean tuna fish is filled with mercury from power plants? My sense of outrage made me feel like I had to do something. If not me, then who? The time for pretending that all was well was over.

I remember having a lunch with John Adams when I poured my heart out and complained that I cared about too many things and I wasn't having an impact on fixing any of them. John advised me to focus on one thing only, the mother of all issues: global warming. And that is exactly what I did.

The good news is it is not all on my or your shoulders. My wise friend Arianna Huffington gave me some great advice, which probably comes from an old Greek proverb, knowing her: Do your 10 percent 100 percent and God will do the other 90 percent. Some mornings, when the problem seems too big or progress too small, I often repeat that to myself. You do not have to do everything, but you have to do something.

As you are reading this right now, there are more than 130 new coal plants under development in the United States, none of which plan to use the clean technology that is currently available. (Voluntary measures don't work!) One new power plant a week goes up in China. When they are built, they will be guaranteeing our carbon emissions for the next sixty years. It doesn't matter if the pollution comes from there or from New York, it all ends up evenly around the planet. Cars and SUVs built today with low fuel-economy standards will be on the road for the next decade, at least. (More than 4 million SUVs are sold in the United States each year, and there are roughly 30 million registered SUVs on American roads.) Decisions are being made today that you are going to deeply resent in just a few years. Feel the burden of that knowledge and change the way you think and help change the way others think. You have a choice to make right now about whether to go forward with business as usual or whether to join the movement for change.

> "Because I care about Mother Earth, animals, people, families, blue skies, the air I breathe, the water I drink, and because health, that of the Earth and her inhabitants, is the most important thing in the short time we are privileged to be here for."
> —Mary Chapin Carpenter

You have the power as individuals and as a generation. What kind of car will you be driving? One that sits you up high but gets fifteen miles to the gallon, or a hybrid that gets forty-five miles per gallon? Will you be a Virtual Marcher? Will you help save the polar bear? Will you protect nature's intentions—snowy winters and livable summers? Will you be brave enough to face the truth? Will you be an activist? You need to decide and you need to decide today. The solution is you!

Afterword

One Girl Saves the World

Laurie David is living proof that one person can make a difference.

In April 2005, just before Earth Day, Laurie told me that she was going to devote all her energies for a single year to changing the national debate about global warming. She was outraged that the public dialogue was focused on whether or not global warming was real, rather than on what America should do to solve it.

"We need to infiltrate popular culture!" she told me. In order to reach a broad swath of American people, Laurie launched the Stop Global Warming Virtual March, behind which people would mobilize a simple nonpartisan demand: our elected leaders in Washington must acknowledge the reality of global warming and act to combat it. She passed over the usual suspects in selecting prominent people to lead the Virtual March. Instead of recruiting environmental leaders and liberal Democrats, she drafted Republican Senator John McCain and Republican Governor Arnold Schwarzenegger; John Hess, chairman of Hess Oil Company; two NFL teams; a bevy of evangelical preachers; and the Indy Racing League.

More than seventy companies, organizations, and sports teams partnered on the March, including AOL, which on its welcome screen encouraged its subscribers to join and incorporated the March into its site through various channels. MTV's college network, mtvU, joined the March and launched a nationwide contest called *Curb Global Warming,*

Win Larry David's Hybrid. This contest reached 8 million students across the country.

Clif Bar put the Stop Global Warming Virtual March logo on its wrappers. Stonyfield Farms put the March on 10 million yogurt lids. Patagonia e-mailed the Stop Global Warming Virtual March to nearly 400,000 customers.

The Philadelphia Eagles and the Saint Louis Rams not only joined the Virtual March, they played the first carbon-neutral green game against each other on December 18, 2005, and encouraged fans and viewers to join the March. Using renewable energy sources to heat and light the dome, the teams offset about fifty-eight tons of CO_2 pollution. Laurie and I participated in the halftime ceremonies honoring the teams' efforts to stop global warming.

Through television, film, and magazines, which Laurie recognized as the fulcrum of popular culture, her global warming message has reached 1.1 million viewers (*The Heat Is On*, Fox news special); several million moviegoers (*An Inconvenient Truth*); 4 million fashion readers (*Elle* magazine's May 2006 green issue, which was the highest selling May issue in fourteen years); 5 million homes (*Earth to America!*, TBS comedy special); 29 million readers (*TIME* magazine's April 2006 issue); 45 million daytime viewers (*The Bold and the Beautiful* soap opera); and 49 million people (*The Oprah Winfrey Show*).

"Laurie David has done more than any one person I know to raise public awareness of the climate crisis," Vice President Al Gore told me. "It was her idea to make a movie from my slide show and it was Laurie who had the drive and determination to recruit a world-class team of movie-industry professionals who were all essential to the film's success. Without her, there simply never would have been a movie. And while she was doing all of this, she continued writing her influential blog, and continued her seemingly constant button-holing of editors and reporters and opinion leaders to push them to do more to cover the global warming issue."

An Inconvenient Truth broke multiple box-office records when it opened to the public on Memorial Day weekend. It was the best-reviewed movie of 2006. Film critic Roger Ebert said, "In thirty-nine years, I have never written these words in a movie review, but here they are: you owe it to yourself to see this film. If you do not and you have grandchildren, you should explain to them why you decided not to."

When President Bush declared that he would not see the Gore movie, he was ridiculed by the late-night hosts. David Letterman cracked that Cheney was so annoyed by the movie that he shot a projectionist. Jay Leno had Bush saying that he didn't need to see the movie because he'd already seen the global-warming cartoon *Ice Age: The Meltdown.*

I really began to appreciate the extent to which Laurie had penetrated the popular culture with her global-warming message when my kids and I, while flipping through the channels one evening in April 2006, happened across an entire South Park episode dedicated to Laurie David and hybrid cars.

And, of course, all those shows generated hundreds of radio shows, TV news coverage, and newspaper and magazine stories in which the issue of global warming was discussed again and again and again. Pretty soon, the most important issue in history even began to penetrate the real news! The mainstream media gave Americans a brief break from Brangelina to discuss global warming!

Now, I'm not saying that all of this has turned around because of the efforts of one lady. Laurie, unfortunately, had help from another powerful lady named Hurricane Katrina, which brought the tragic real-world costs of global warming home in a fury to the American people.

I grew up surrounded by powerful, wonderful women. Among them were my grandmother, mother of three U.S. senators and the president of the United States; my Aunt Eunice Shriver, founder of the Special Olympics; my Aunt Jean Smith, the former ambassador to Ireland; my elder sister

Kathleen, who was lieutenant governor of Maryland; my sister Kerry, a leading human-rights activist; and my youngest sister, Rory, who is an Oscar-nominated documentary-film producer. But I've never met anyone quite like Laurie David. Laurie is sui generis. She has shown us all that even on the most intractable issues, one stubborn individual can change the national paradigm. "If a single man plants himself firmly upon his own ideal, and there abide," Emerson wrote, "the whole wide world will come round to him." Laurie would be Emerson's "exhibit A." Before that breathtaking year, Laurie had never produced a network show, written a book, made a speech, or organized the grass roots. She reinvented herself as an activist and forced herself to learn all these skills and focus them like a laser on global warming. As *Elle* magazine editorialized, "If you meet Laurie you won't forget her. Smart, passionate, deeply stylish, and, thank God, funny, she has an elegantly simple ethos: Pick one thing, just one thing, that you can do to improve the environment."

But the secret of her effectiveness comes from a clear ambitious vision, boundless energy, and her tough, strategic mind. Her sense of diplomacy and endearing charm disarm even those inclined by politics or prejudice to dislike her— staunch Republicans, for example, such as Roger Ailes or Joe Scarborough. But her most potent weapon is the persuasiveness and confidence that come from an utterly selfless passion. Laurie believes we are saving the planet for our children. She simply cannot believe that everyone wouldn't also make this their issue. I once asked her how she had the guts to cold-call these big shots in politics, business, and entertainment— whom she didn't know—and ask them to do favors. She told me, "I know in my heart that I have no agenda here other than saving the planet. I don't have any hesitation or fear about demanding that everyone do their part!"

We may not all have the volcanic energy of Laurie David, but we can all do something to be effective in our own communities. That's how the globe will be saved. We need to create activists in every corner of America doing the same work Laurie has done in Hollywood and New York. Now she has given us the tools: the Gore movie, *An Inconvenient Truth*, which we can watch to educate ourselves; the Virtual March, which allows all of us to take the first step in activism; and this book, which is a blueprint for effective advocacy.

We have a role model, we have a plan. Let's get started!

—Robert F. Kennedy Jr.

Resources

Books

Bourseiller, Philippe. *365 Ways to Save the Earth*. New York: Harry N. Abrams, 2005.

Bradsher, Keith. *High and Mighty: SUVs: The World's Most Dangerous Vehicles and How They Got That Way*. New York: Public Affairs, 2002.

Diamond, Jared. *Collapse: How Societies Choose to Fail or Succeed*. New York: Viking, 2005.

Flannery, Tim. *The Weather Makers: How Man Is Changing the Climate and What It Means for Life on Earth*. New York: Atlantic Monthly, 2005.

Gelbspan, Ross. *Boiling Point: How Politicians, Big Oil and Coal, Journalists, and Activists Are Fueling the Climate Crisis—And What We Can Do to Avert Disaster*. New York: Basic Books, 2004.

Goodell, Jeff. *Big Coal: The Dirty Secret behind America's Energy Future*. Boston: Houghton Mifflin, 2006.

Gore, Al. *An Inconvenient Truth: The Planetary Emergency of Global Warming and What We Can Do About It*. Emmaus, PA: Rodale Press, 2006.

———. *Earth in the Balance: Ecology and the Human Spirit*. Boston: Houghton Mifflin, 2000.

Hertsgaard, Mark. *Earth Odyssey: Around the World in Search of Our Environmental Future*. New York: Broadway Books, 1998.

Kennedy Jr., Robert F. *Crimes against Nature: How George W. Bush and His Corporate Pals Are*

Plundering the Country and Hijacking Our Democracy. New York: HarperCollins, 2004.

Kolbert, Elizabeth. *Field Notes from a Catastrophe: Man, Nature, and Climate Change.* New York: Bloomsbury Pub., 2006.

McKibben, Bill. *The End of Nature.* New York: Anchor Books, 1990.

Revkin, Andrew. *The North Pole Was Here: Puzzles and Perils at the Top of the World.* New York: Kingfisher, 2006.

Speth, James Gustave. *Red Sky at Morning: America and the Crisis of the Global Environment—A Citizen's Agenda for Action.* New Haven: Yale Univ. Press, 2004.

Wilkinson, Todd. *Science under Siege: The Politicians' War on Nature and Truth.* Boulder, CO: Johnson Books, 1998.

DVDs

60 Minutes: Rewriting the Science
An Inconvenient Truth
Global Warming: The Signs and the Science
Too Hot NOT to Handle
Who Killed the Electric Car?

Web sites

www.cleartheair.org—"Clear the Air is a national public education campaign to combat global warming."

www.climateark.org—"Climate Change and Global Warming Portal"

www.climatecrisis.net—Resource for *An Inconvenient Truth*

www.climatehotmap.org—Features a map that illustrates the local consequences of global warming.

www.climatesciencewatch.org—"Climate Science Watch is a nonprofit public-interest education and advocacy project dedicated to holding public officials accountable for the integrity and effectiveness with which they use climate science and related research in government policy making, toward the goal of enabling society to respond effectively to the challenges posed by global warming and climate change."

www.grist.org—Grist is fiercely independent in covering environmental news. It is focused on telling the untold stories, spotlighting trends, and educating people about the environment.

www.huffingtonpost.com

www.idealbite.com—"The concept behind Ideal Bite is an easy one: if we all knew what to do in our day-to-day lives to help impact the planet and our communities positively and painlessly (and without preachiness), we would all do it."

www.powerscorecard.org—"The Power Scorecard is a rating mechanism that assesses the environmental impact of different types of electric generation. The Power Scorecard makes it easy for you to plug into cleaner power for the future of the planet."

www.realclimate.org—"Real Climate is a commentary site on climate science by working climate scientists for the interested public and journalists."

www.stopglobalwarming.org

www.treehugger.com—"Treehugger is a fast-growing Internet magazine, dedicated to everything that has a modern aesthetic yet is environmentally responsible."

www.worldviewofglobalwarming.org—Highlights global warming at the extremes of the Earth. Habitats and cultures everywhere react to climate's rapid changes.

Reduce, Reuse, and Recycle

www.buyenergyefficient.org—The Consumer Federation of America's checklist of 10 Simple Ways to Cut Home Energy Costs and other suggestions to reduce your greenhouse gas emissions.

www.climatebiz.com/sections/news_detail.cfm?newsid =27338—Learn about eating local and how it fights global warming.

www.earth911.org/master.asp?s=ls&a=recycle&cat=1 or www.epa.gov/epaoswer/non-hw/muncpl/recycle .htm—Learn where you can recycle in your area.

www.environmentaldefense.org/article.cfm?contentid= 2194—Learn about how to reduce waste before you buy, such as choosing items with less packaging and buying in bulk.

www.epa.gov/compost/index.htm or www.master composter.com—Learn about composting.

www.epa.gov/msw/reduce.htm—Learn how to reduce, reuse, and recycle.

www.freecycle.org—Learn how to give away something you no longer need.

www.grrn.org/beverage/refillables/index.html—Learn about the benefits of using refillable beverage containers.

www.newdream.org/junkmail or www.dmaconsumers .org/offmailinglist.html—Learn how to remove your name from mailing lists.

www.newdream.org—Ideas on how to consume less.

www.reusablebags.com—To purchase reusable bags, learn bag facts, and find out about actions you can take.

Energy Use in the Home

www.aceee.org/consumerguide/chklst.htm—Learn to properly operate and maintain your appliances by reviewing a checklist and extensive FAQ.

www.awea.org/faq/netbdef.html—Learn about net-metering (when a household produces its own clean energy by photovoltaic cells, wind energy, or geothermal heat pumps and sells their surplus energy back to the utility).

www.dsireusa.org—Learn about state and local governments and utility companies that offer personal tax credits or subsidies for renewable energy projects.

www.eere.energy.gov (consumer/renewable energy), www.ases.org (solar energy), and www.awea.org (wind energy)—Learn about renewable power.

www.eere.energy.gov/greenpower—If you cannot install your own renewable energy, your region may have the option for you to contract with your utility company to receive energy from more environmentally friendly sources.

www.energyguide.com—This site contains a do-it-yourself energy audit that will help identify areas of your home that are consuming the most energy.

www.energystar.gov/products—Learn about energy-efficient appliances. Visit www.energystar.gov/index.cfm?=ofc_equip.pr_office_equipment to learn about Energy Star office equipment.

www.green-e.org—If green energy is not available through your public utility, you have the option of purchasing Tradeable Renewable Certificates (TRCs) to offset your energy use.

www.natresnet.org/directory/rater_directory.asp#serach—Use this site to find an energy specialist in your area. You can also contact your utility company or state energy office.

www.simplyinsulate.com—Learn about insulating your house.

www.standby.lbl.gov/index.html—Learn about standby, or phantom, energy.

Reduce Your Transportation Emissions

www.afdc.doe.gov/advanced_cgi.shtml—Learn about alternative fuels.

www.americawalks.org—Learn about lobbying for better walking conditions.

www.betterworldclub.com/travel/index.htm—Offers help for planning green travel and purchasing carbon offsets.

www.bikeleague.org—Learn about lobbying for better biking conditions.

www.epa.gov/autoemissions or www.fueleconomy.gov—Learn about miles-per-gallon estimates for most cars.

www.fueleconomy.gov/feg/driveHabits.shtml—Learn about maximizing the fuel efficiency of your car.

www.hybridcars.com—Learn about hybrids cars—how they work and the various models.

www.publictransportation.org—Learn how to use and support public transportation.

www.telcoa.org—Learn about telecommuting.

The Power of Your Pocketbook and the Ballot

www.ci.seattle.wa.us/mayor/climate—Learn about the U.S. Mayors Climate Protection Agreement.

www.coopamerica.org/programs/responsibleshopper—Learn about the environmental practices and policies of the businesses that make the products you buy.

www.lcv.org/scorecard—Learn where politicians stand on global warming.

www.socialinvest.org—Offers comprehensive information, contacts, and resources on socially responsible investing.

Environmental Groups

1% for the Planet—"A network of more than 150 members that commit to giving 1 percent of their revenues to environmental organizations every year." Phone: 1-978-462-5353; Web site: www.onepercent fortheplanet.org

3 Phases Energy Services—"At 3 Phases Energy, our mission is to create or stimulate the creation of 100% renewable energy in our lifetimes as part of a

cleaner, more renewable world." Phone: 1-866-476-9378 (toll-free); Web site: www.3phases.com

Acterra—"To create local solutions that foster a healthy natural environment." Phone: 1-650-962-9876; Web site: www.acterra.org

The Aspen Global Warming Alliance—"We're trying to engage the business community, and say global warming is an environmental problem. But it's also an economic problem." Phone: 1-970-920-5075; Web site: www.aspenglobalwarming.com

Better World Club—The nation's greener, cooler auto club. "Admittedly, 'coolness' is subjective, but certainly when it comes to global warming: we're the coolest source for emergency roadside assistance in the U.S." Phone: 1-866-238-1137; Web site: www.betterworldclub.com

Bioneers—"Bioneers is a nonprofit organization that promotes practical environmental solutions and innovative social strategies for restoring the Earth and communities." Phone: 1-877-BIONEER; Web site: www.bioneers.org

Bonneville Environmental Foundation—"The Bonneville Environmental Foundation is a charitable and non-profit public benefit corporation dedicated to encouraging and funding activities and projects that lead to greater reliance on clean, environmentally preferred renewable power, and to healthy sustainable fish and wildlife habitat within the Pacific Northwest." Phone: 1-866-BEF-TAGS; Web site: www.b-e-f.org

CALPIRG—"Through CALPIRG, students gain an educational experience in democratic citizenship. In addition, we get a chance to face up to society's big problems, take action, and win concrete changes that improve the quality of our lives." Phone: 1-213-251-3680; Web site: www.calpirgstudents.org

CarbonFund.org—"Carbonfund.org reduces the threat of climate change by making it easy and affordable for any individual or business to reduce their carbon footprint and support climate-friendly projects. Please take action today!" Phone: 1-240-556-1908; Web site: www.carbonfund.org

Care2—"Our goal is 'Make the world a better place by connecting people who care (that's you!) with the organizations, responsible businesses and individuals getting results. It's a big plan that touches on health, the environment, women's rights, spirituality, children's welfare, human rights and much more.'" Phone: 1-650-622-0860; Web site: www.care2.com

Center for Biological Diversity—"The Center for Biological Diversity works to protect the diversity of life on Earth. We believe that our lives are immeasurably enriched by the millions of non-human species with which we share this planet and diminished when ecosystems are degraded and species become extinct." Phone: 1-520-623-5252; Web site: www.biologicaldiversity.org

Chesapeake Climate Action Network—"The Chesapeake Climate Action Network (CCAN) is the first grass-roots, nonprofit organization dedicated exclusively to fighting global warming in Maryland, Virginia, and Washington, D.C. Our mission is to educate and mobilize citizens of this region in a way that fosters a rapid societal switch to clean energy and energy-efficient products, thus joining similar efforts worldwide to slow and perhaps halt the dangerous trend of global warming." Phone: 1-301-891-6844; Web site: www.chesapeakeclimate.org

Clean Air–Cool Planet—"Clean Air–Cool Planet creates partnerships in the Northeast to implement solutions to climate change and build constituencies for effective climate policies and actions." Phone:

1-603-422-6464; Web site: www.cleanair-cool
planet.org

CleanAirPass—"Cleanairpass is committed to making it
easy for people to take responsibility for the personal
greenhouse gas emissions they create, and give
them a way to help the growth of the renewable
energy industry at the same time." Phone: 1-800-
601-0724; Web site: www.cleanairpass.com

Coalition on the Environmental and Jewish Life—
"COEJL has put environmental protection on the
agenda of the organized Jewish community and
made the case to elected officials and decision-
makers that protecting the environment is a moral
and religious obligation." Phone: 1-212-532-7436;
Web site: www.coejl.org

The Conservation Alliance—"The Conservation Alliance
is an organization of outdoor businesses whose
collective contributions support grassroots conservation organizations and their efforts to protect
wild places where outdoor enthusiasts recreate."
Phone: 1-541-388-4845; Web site: www.conservation
alliance.com

The Conservation Fund—"The Conservation Fund, a
national environmental nonprofit, has been a recognized leader in developing and implementing
'on-the-ground' solutions to help fight global
warming." Phone: 1-703-525-6300; Web site:
www.conservationfund.org

Conservation International—"Conservation International
is a non-partisan organization working with communities, the private sector, and governments
worldwide to protect Earth's natural riches—its
biological diversity—that make up the delicately
balanced ecosystems we depend on for our sur-
vival." Phone: 1-800-406-2306; Web site: www
.conservation.org

Coral Reef Alliance—"The Coral Reef Alliance is dedicated to protecting the health of coral reefs by uniting ecosystem management, sustainable tourism, and community partnerships." Phone: 1-888-CORAL-REEF; Web site: www.coralreefalliance.org

Defenders of Wildlife—"Defenders of Wildlife is dedicated to the protection of all native wild animals and plants in their natural communities." Phone: 1-800-385-9712; Web site: www.defenders.org

DriveNeutral—"DriveNeutral helps ease the tension between our commitment to create a better future and our need to drive ourselves to work, school and the store." Phone: 1-415-561-1170; Web site: www.driveneutral.com

E2 Environmental Entrepreneurs—"E2 (Environmental Entrepreneurs) is a national network of business people who believe that environmental progress and economic growth go hand-in-hand." Phone: 1-415-875-6100; Web site: www.e2.org

Earth Share—"Earth Share is also a nonpartisan organization that recognizes the importance of promoting awareness about urgent environmental issues such as global warming to help protect our health, well-being, and the future of our natural heritage." Phone: 1-800-875-3863; Web site: www.earthshare.org

Earthship Biotecture—"Earthship Biotecture, based in Taos, NM, USA, is a global company offering proven, totally sustainable designs, construction drawings and details, products, educational materials, lectures/presentations, consultation and guidance toward getting people in sustainable housing. From single family to colony/community/city complexes." Phone: 1-505-751-0462; Web site: www.earthship.org

EcoDesignz—"We wanted to give the global economy an alternative away from deforestation for flooring and furniture, as well as clothing, by providing these goods in a beautiful, sustainable material, bamboo." Phone: 1-310-538-3051; Web site: www.ecodesignz.com

EcoMall—"EcoMall provides information and resources to become politically active in environmental issues, as well as network with other people, organizations and companies who support the environment, building a powerful collective movement and providing a sense of community." Phone: 1-845-679-2490; Web site: www.ecomall.com

Energy Action—"Energy Action is a coalition of 25 leading student environmental and social justice organizations in the U.S. and Canada created to unify and support the student global warming and clean energy movement." Phone: 1-203-887-7225; Web site: www.energyaction.net

Energy Federation Incorporated—"Through the distribution of resource-conserving products and the provision of objective, accurate information, we strive to assist people in their efforts to use energy and water efficiently." Phone: 1-508-870-2277; Web site: www.efi.org

Environmental Media Association—"The Environmental Media Association (EMA) mobilizes the entertainment industry in a global effort to educate people about environmental issues and inspire them into action." Phone: 1-310-446-6244; Web site: www.ema-online.org

Environmental Defense Fund—"Since 1967, we have linked science, economics and law to create innovative, equitable and cost-effective solutions to society's most urgent environmental problems." Phone: 1-212-505-2100; Web site: www.environmental defense.org

EnvironmentPunk.com—EnvironmentPunk.com is trying to do its part by spreading the message behind preserving the environment to the thousands of people that use the Internet. Web site: www.envi ronmentpunk.com

ERideShare.com—A free national service available to help you coordinate your travels with other commuters. Phone: 1-618-530-4842; Web site: www .erideshare.com

The Evergreen Group—"The Evergreen Group is the only business brokerage in the country dedicated to helping green-business owners sell their businesses to like-minded buyers. We facilitate smooth and successful transfers of ownership of socially and environmentally sustainable businesses." Phone: 1-415-750-1120; Web site: www.theevergreengroup.com

Friends of the Earth—"Friends of the Earth has for decades been at the forefront of high-profile efforts to create a more healthy, just world." Phone: 1-415-544-0790; Web site: www.foe.org

Global Warming Action Coalition—Lexington—"The mission of the Global Warming Action Coalition—Lexington is to educate and to raise awareness about global warming and climate change, and to promote actions on the part of individual citizens and our town government to reduce greenhouse gas emissions and develop sustainable practices throughout the town of Lexington." Web site: www.lexgwac.org

GreenLeap—"GreenLeap's mission is to inform and inspire individuals who share care and concern for wildlife, nature and the environment in which we live." Web site: www.greenleap.com

HybridCars.com—Contains information on researching and buying hybrids..

League of Conservation Voters—"The League of Conservation Voters (LCV) is the political voice of the national environmental movement and the only organization devoted full-time to shaping a pro-environment Congress and White House." Phone: 1-202-785-8683; Web site: www.lcv.org

National Association of Environmental Law Societies— "The National Association of Environmental Law Societies (NAELS) is a coalition of over 50 law student groups that aims to connect, educate, and inspire the next generation of environmental leaders." Phone: 1-314-569-1615; Web site: www.naels.org

National Wildlife Federation—"Our organization is committed to protecting wildlife for our children's future—a mission that puts global warming front and center on our list of issues to tackle." Phone: 1-800-822-9919; Web site: www.nwf.org

Native Energy—"NativeEnergy is working with forward-thinking businesses and individuals to get more safe and pollution-free wind, solar, and biomass energy projects up and running." Phone: 1-800-924-6826; Web site: www.nativeenergy.com

Natural Resources Defense Council—"NRDC is the nation's most effective environmental action organization. We use law, science and the support of 1.2 million members and online activists to protect the planet's wildlife and wild places and to ensure a safe and healthy environment for all living things." Phone: 1-212-727-2700; Web site: www.nrdc.org

Oceana—"Oceana campaigns to protect and restore the world's oceans." Phone: 1-310-899-3026; Web site: www.oceana.org

Organic.org—"At Organic.org, we are not only committed to the benefits of organic growing and the resulting products, but also to an organic mindset." Web site: www.organic.org

OurEnergy.us—"OurEnergy is the only program that allows you to support the generation of clean

American renewable energy at absolutely no cost to you." Web site: www.ourenergy.us

Post Carbon Institute—"Post Carbon Institute supports and partners with initiatives that are working to stop climate change and mitigate the effects that have affected humans all across the globe." Phone: 1-604-736-9000; Web site: www.postcarbon.org

Rainforest Action Network—"Rainforest Action Network campaigns for the forests, their inhabitants and the natural systems that sustain life by transforming the global marketplace through education, grassroots organizing, and nonviolent direct action." Phone: 1-415-398-4404; Web site: www.ran.org

Rainforest Alliance—"The mission of the Rainforest Alliance is to protect ecosystems and the people and wildlife that depend on them by transforming land-use practices, business practices and consumer behavior." Phone: 1-888-MY-EARTH; Web site: www.rainforest-alliance.org

Restoring Eden—"Restoring Eden makes hearts bigger, hands dirtier, and voices stronger by encouraging Christians to learn to love, serve, and protect God's creation." Phone: 1-360-574-8230; Web site: www.restoringeden.org

SaveOurEnvironment.org—"Saveourenvironment.org harnesses the power of the Internet to increase public awareness and activism on today's most important environmental issues." Web site: www.saveourenvironment.org

Sierra Club—"The Sierra Club's members are more than 750,000 of your friends and neighbors. Inspired by nature, we work together to protect our communities and the planet. The Club is America's oldest, largest and most influential grassroots environmental organization." Phone: 1-415-977-5500; Web site: www.sierraclub.org

Smarttransportation.org—"SmartTransportation.org is dedicated to improving the health of New Yorkers through smarttransportation.org solutions. We are a coaliton of health, civic and environmental organizations working together to improve our lives through such innovations as hybrid taxis and buses." Phone: 1-917-621-7167; Web site: www.smarttransportation.org

Sterling Planet—"Sterling Planet's mission is to lead the migration to sustainable energy that is good for the environment, the economy and all current and future generations." Phone: 1-678-325-3170; Web site: www.sterlingplanet.com

Union of Concerned Scientists—"The Union of Concerned Scientists is the leading science-based nonprofit working for a healthy environment and a safer world. UCS combines independent scientific research and citizen action to develop innovative, practical solutions and to secure responsible changes in government policy, corporate practices, and consumer choices." Phone: 1-617-547-5552; Web site: www.ucsusa.org

Vivavi—"Vivavi was founded to bring environmental consciousness to contemporary design in order to promote and preserve the highest quality of life for current and future generations. Every product we offer tells a story about increased environmental awareness, made from pure and renewable and recycled and resource-efficient materials." Phone: 1-866-848-2840; Web site: www.vivavi.com

Acknowledgments

Writing a book is a unique challenge and can only really be met with the help of many. First and foremost, I need to thank my wonderful associate Dawn Woollen, who sweetly and professionally went through every single draft with me from start to finish and was a wonderful sounding board for ideas, amplifications, and suggestions. Many thanks also to the Stop Global Warming team: Liana, Lindsay, Heather, Brendan DeMelle (ace researcher), Lisa Chase (ace volunteer editor), Kathy Bega, Susan Hassol, and Frances Bienecke, who makes sure the brilliant staff of the Natural Resources Defense Council is always available. Special thanks to NRDC's David Hawkins, Jon Coifman, David Tuft, John Steelman, and Allen Hershkowitz; as well as Mark Seliger, photograher extraordinaire, who shot the cover for us as a favor and on a week's notice; Rhoda Boone, who produced the shoot; and Cami Gordon, for her constant friendship, support, and great advice. Special thanks also to Arianna Huffington for nonstop inspiration, the Huffington Post for hosting my global warming tirades, and Roy Sekoff for always making sure my tirades are coherent. And lastly, my editor, Sam Scinta, who convinced me to write a book in the first place by promising me it only had to be about ninety-six pages long.